Church alive!

Church alive!
A fresh look at Church Growth

Peter Cotterell

Inter-Varsity Press

Inter-Varsity Press
38 De Montfort Street, Leicester LE1 7GP, England
© PETER COTTERELL 1981

Unless otherwise stated, quotations from the Bible are from the
Revised Standard Version, copyrighted 1946, 1952, © 1971, 1973
by the Division of the Churches of Christ in the USA,
and used by permission.

First published 1981
Reprinted 1983

British Library Cataloguing in Publication Data
Cotterell, Peter
Church alive!
1. Church renewal
I. Title
262'0017   BV600.2

ISBN 0-85110-431-2

Set in 10/11pt Linotype Times and 9/10 Univers
Typeset in Great Britain by Nuprint Services Ltd, Harpenden, Herts
Printed in bound in Great Britain by
Collins, Glasgow

*Inter-Varsity Press is the publishing division of the Universities and
Colleges Christian Fellowship (formerly the Inter-Varsity Fellowship),
a student movement linking Christian Unions in universities and
colleges throughout the British Isles, and a member movement of the
International Fellowship of Evangelical Students. For information
about local and national activities in Great Britain write to
UCCF, 38 De Montfort Street, Leicester LE1 7GP.*

D, L and E

I believe that it is largely our fault that so many churches in Britain are dull, lifeless and...empty. Yes, I *know* that there are some exciting churches where they're doing everything right. If you come from one of them, well, God bless you. Give this book to someone else. You don't need it. But if you come from a dull, lifeless and...empty church, *read on!*

Because if I am right and it is largely our fault that so many churches are D, L and E, then there is hope for us. We can do something about it.

This book isn't written for scholars to review but for church people to use. I don't want to start a debate or found a new school of thought. I want to help to bring dead churches to life. This is a kind of ideas book for concerned Christians. I don't want to see people leaving their churches and going off to start something else. I'm *for* the church. I believe that God wants new life in the churches and I've seen it happen. In the most unlikely places. Yes, I've known D, L and E churches and I've seen them come alive.

But it won't happen unless we are prepared to foot the bill. Too often ministers (yes, especially ministers) and the rest of us aren't prepared to do it. To give the money to up-date church seating and to install some decent lighting. To give time to meeting people in our homes rather than attending non-meetings in our churches. To think about what's being done. To pray about what *should* be done.

It doesn't really make sense to read this book on your own. It needs to be read aloud with other people from your church, because it is a *church* book. And as you read together, *pray* together that somehow God will take D, L and E churches – your church? – and bring new life to them.

Contents

1
This is where we start

I first came into contact with the Church Growth movement back in 1968. Although I had read very little about the movement I already had it labelled 'Dangerous'. The name itself told me all I needed to know: it was obviously just another American system for getting round the sovereignty of the Holy Spirit and saving souls by the barrow-load.

But now I know better. Church Growth is not merely one more system of evangelism. It is not a method guaranteed to grow churches painlessly. In fact it isn't a method at all. It *is* a *movement,* almost a spontaneous movement, of Christians who are concerned to see the churches getting back to right, biblical priorities. Put at its simplest, Church Growth thinking says that any church that is not seeing people being saved, coming to Christ, being discipled into the church, being born again, ought to be concerned to ask, 'Why not?'

The movement is not entirely spontaneous. It owes most to Dr Donald McGavran, who was a missionary in India. He was concerned at mission practice which took people who were converted *out of* their own environment, out of the usual run of Indian village or city life, and isolated them on mission 'stations'. It was all done for the very best of reasons: life in Hindu society for a Christian convert was extremely difficult. So new converts tended to be skimmed off and turned into mission employees. They were isolated. Instead of being bridges they became islands. So McGavran wrote his first book, *The bridges of God,* usually taken to be the starting-point for his thinking on Church Growth.

That was a beginning. At first Church Growth thinking developed in terms of mission work overseas. But in the early 1970s questions began to be asked about the relevance of Church Growth thinking to the church back at home. Tentatively to begin with, and then with growing enthusiasm, the movement spread. And rather late in time the concepts began to emerge in Europe, too.

It seems to me that the movement reached us at exactly the right time. By the end of the 1970s the church in Europe was heaving itself out of the long years of depression. The Spirit of God was beginning to be heard once again. New opportunities for speaking about Jesus began to appear. Church after church was demanding a new look at what was being done. In a general economic collapse and a general moral vacuum all kinds of exciting opportunities faced the church. Church Growth, properly presented, made good sense. But in Britain the movement had its critics, and it had to overcome the disadvantage of its American origin. In particular there was the fundamental question to be settled: is it biblical?

Two basic presuppositions

Church Growth thinking, as it is presented in this book, has two vital presuppositions. It is failure to make these presuppositions clear that has caused so much misunderstanding of what Church Growth has to say.

The first basic presupposition is that we accept *the total authority of the Bible.* This does need to be spelt out clearly. It does not mean merely that I believe what is in the Bible, or even merely that I believe that what is in the Bible is the Word of God. It means that I accept the *authority* of the

Bible. The Bible comes first and my own ideas, or the ideas of sociology or whatever, come later. I am not a pragmatist. Pragmatism is doing something simply because it seems to work, because doing it *this* way produces the desired result. Or, at least it *seems* to produce the desired result. I would reject pragmatism: Scripture comes first.

So then, if I find that a certain approach to church life has the result of filling the church, but that the approach appears to be contrary to biblical teaching, then I reject that approach. You can fill the church for all the wrong reasons and with all the wrong people. You could probably fill the church by offering free coffee and doughnuts after a shortened morning service. You could probably fill the church by replacing worship with some kind of Christian variety show. But Church Growth is *not* merely a method of filling the church. Church Growth is concerned with the biblically-understood task of the church to be Christ's witnesses and so to see people discipled into Christ and becoming *real* Christians.

This first presupposition about Church Growth raises the question of *hermeneutics,* the scholar's word for describing my presuppositions when I approach the Bible. Now whenever I approach a book I do so with certain expectations, with certain preconceived ideas. These ideas come from what I already know of both the book and its author. I happen to enjoy P.G. Wodehouse. I also enjoy Winston S. Churchill. But I don't approach Churchill's books in the same way as I approach Wodehouse's. I take Churchill seriously but I can't, and indeed I mustn't, take Wodehouse's Bertie Wooster seriously.

When I approach the Bible I do so already knowing a good deal about it. I've been teaching it for a good many years now. As I think about the way I approach the Bible five principles seem to govern my thinking and reading.

a. The Bible is inspired. Uniquely inspired. It is inspired in a way that guarantees not merely its general trustworthiness, but its actual inerrancy. True enough, there are still some problems with regard to the Bible that I've not yet been able to work out, but I'm old enough to have seen many such problems resolved for me and I'm quite prepared to leave the rest to be worked out similarly in God's own time.

The inspiration of the Bible allows for the principle of selection. John tells us this, quite clearly (John 20:30). We do not have Paul's letter to the Laodiceans nor at least one more letter to the Corinthians. But their loss is part of inspiration: they were not meant to be in the Bible.

b. Bible literature is presented in many forms. The Bible comes to us as letters and poems, and as history and law and biography and so on. If I am going to understand the message of the Bible, then I must take the *form* of the message into account.

c. In understanding the Bible attention must also be paid to the *context.* Verses of the Bible must not be lifted out of their context and then applied in a very different context. 'Behold, I stand at the door and knock' (Revelation 3:20), for example, is written in a letter to Christians and ought not to be pulled out of that context and applied to evangelizing people who aren't Christians. Or, if I want teaching about marriage, then I should look at those parts of the Bible which explicitly teach about marriage.

d. I must distinguish between what is *described* in Scripture and what is *prescribed* in Scripture. Much of the Bible is descriptive, not prescriptive. For example, we have a rather full *description* of how Paul carried out mission. But that description does not necessarily *prescribe* how mission ought to be carried out today. Times have changed. Conditions are different. Paul could rely on Greek being spoken wherever he went, while we have to learn new languages as we move from country to country. Paul was a Jew, and so it was possible for him to begin his preaching in the local synagogue. I wouldn't get very far today if I tried to start preaching in a synagogue in Jerusalem!

e. In general I should expect to take the obvious meaning of a passage of the Bible rather than some 'spiritualization' of it. Of course this does mean that I shall have to take the time to try to discover what the obvious meaning of the passage was to the first readers of it. And that might well mean that I should have to give time to studying history and language and culture. I have to recognize that the 'obvious' meaning is often not quite as obvious as I might have thought it to be. We are immensely fortunate to have plenty of readable books by Christians who have done the groundwork for us.

The second basic presupposition is *the sovereignty of the Holy Spirit.* I cannot tell him what to do, whom to save, how many to save. I cannot demand that certain spiritual gifts should be given to particular individuals in particular churches. Church Growth recognizes the sovereignty of the Spirit. It does not offer a method that can short-circuit him.

But what Church Growth thinking often can do is to remove obstacles to the working of the Spirit. If the Holy Spirit has given certain gifts to the members of my church, and if I have a mistaken view of the one-man type of ministry, then I may block the work of the Spirit by making it impossible for those gifts to be used. If there is someone in the church who has a gift of teaching, but I feel that I must do all the teaching because I am the minister, then I hinder the Spirit. Church Growth thinking may be used to make the minister of such a church realize his mistake and then to open the way for the gifts to be used. In Church Growth thinking there is no intention at all to circumvent the work of the Spirit. Rather the intention is to set him free to carry out his unique and indispensable work.

So these are the two basic presuppositions of the Church Growth movement: the authority of the Bible and the sovereignty of the Spirit. It would be very monotonous to re-state these two presuppositions each time any proposal was being made about ways of discipling people into the

13

church. That is why they are introduced here, at the beginning of the book. Even so, I'm fairly sure that some people will read the book and miss these presuppositions. I can't do very much about that except, perhaps, to slip in a reminder every so often with the letters SS. These simply mean 'Scripture and Spirit'. It is a reminder that these two presuppositions do lie behind all that is being said, and that there is no suggestion being made that we can go beyond them.

Two principles of group relationships

It is amazing to observe how very differently people behave when they are alone, when they are with husband or wife, when they are with a small group of friends or when they are with a crowd. Our behaviour is affected by the people we are with. It is important to notice that human beings are naturally gregarious: we like to meet in groups. The local church is just one of the natural groups which we experience.

Now groups meet only when they have some reason for meeting. An orchestra meets in order to play music. A sailing club meets in order to sail. As long as the members of the orchestra have the opportunity of playing together and the members of the sailing club have the opportunity of sailing, they will continue to meet. But if they can't, they won't. If they can't play music or they can't sail boats, then they won't meet.

So, an important principle of group behaviour is that *for any group to continue to exist as a group it must have a primary task*. This is the first of two important principles which lie behind group relationships. The church is a group, so that if a local church is to continue to exist it must have a primary task to perform. If there is no genuine task for the church to perform it will cease to function as a group. Let me explain. A short while ago I was visiting a language school. While I was there the fire-alarm sounded. At once a group of students appeared and gathered around the doorway of the hut from which the fire-alarm had sounded. They were the camp's fire-fighters, so they had a primary task: to put out the fire. However, it was soon discovered that, as usual, it was a false alarm. There was no fire. Since there was no fire there was no task for the group. And so the group split up.

There is a second important principle that helps to explain group relationships, and this second principle is also of great importance for the church: *within any group a subgroup* (sometimes called by specialists 'the basic assumptions group') *will eventually emerge which will attempt to replace the primary task of the group by a substitute task*.

This example is taken from an article by P.M. Turquet of the Tavistock Institute of Human Relations. A family business had for many years been successfully manufacturing men's clothing. But marketing patterns changed and sales began to sag. There was an obvious need to find some way into the big retail distributing chains. Of course this would mean replacing the company name proudly displayed on every coat produced by the firm. The name of the chain store would have to appear instead. The matter was put to the Board of the company. The suggestion was rejected out of hand: How can we allow our unique product, known by its trusted name-label, to be marketed under someone else's name? The proposal was rejected, sales continued to fall, the firm was finally rescued only by a take-over bid, the Directors lost their seats...and the clothes were manufactured and distributed under the brand name of the chain store.

The fact was that the Directors had lost sight of their primary task, to produce good quality men's clothing in a profitable way, and instead had a substitute task, to promote the name of the company.

This kind of thing regularly happens to churches. The primary task of the church is forgotten and for some reason a substitute task emerges. Instead of being Christ's witnesses in the district we may concentrate on holding services. Through no fault of their own there are vicars whose primary task is raising enough money to have the leaking roof repaired, or even finding enough time to bury the dead of the

15

parish which has trebled in size while the number of clergy has been halved. Ministers may find themselves spending their days pacifying squabbling church members who may have begun their squabbles while engaged in *their* substitute task, the planning of the annual jumble sale. Diaconates may be more concerned with matters of insurance than they are with the assurance of the church members.

Church Growth is concerned to identify the primary task of the church and then to assist churches to extricate themselves from the miscellany of substitute tasks which keep the church busy but ineffective.

NOW WHAT DO WE DO?

1. A basic question: What is the primary task of your church? Take careful note of the question. Not 'What *ought* the primary task to be?' but, 'What *is*...?'

Now how do you find out the answer to this question? Well, take a look first at the church accounts. What is most of the money spent on? Make an honest list. How much on the minister's salary? How much on church heating and cleaning and repairs? And how much on outreach? Anything for tracts or books to give away? Hiring school halls for films? Cost of training weekends?

Then look at your people. What are the church members *doing*? Taking services? Teaching Sunday school? Outreach into British Legion, Rotary Club, youth clubs, schools?

2. Read something. Grove Booklet no. 21 is on evangelistic services, no. 38 is about Parish renewal. Read also the first two chapters of Michael Harper's *Let my people grow*.

Chapter 3 of John Stott's *Our guilty silence* deals with the responsibility of the church for outreach. Note what Stott has to say about Joost de Blank's words: 'Evangelism is the normal life of the church, and can never be an optional extra.' How would you describe evangelism in your church: *normal, seasonal* or *occasional*? What sort of conduct would you expect of church members, what sort of decisions would you expect of your church committees and what sort of activities would you expect in your church if evangelism were to become 'normal'?

3. A certain Sunday school has been operating now for more than forty years. In the last ten years attendance has averaged nearly 100 each week. But almost all the children drop out at about thirteen. Why? Is it worth while continuing the Sunday school? What sort of questions would you ask to enable you to decide what to do about the Sunday school?

4. 'They didn't have choirs in the Bible.' Why is this a wrong application of the idea that what we do must be biblical? (Oh yes, they *do* still use this kind of argument. I heard it only last week, used against music groups rather than choirs. And anyway, what about the choirs mentioned in 1 Chronicles 6 or in Nehemiah 12, for instance?) Can you think of other examples of this kind of muddled thinking? Why do we sometimes argue in this way? Do *you* sometimes argue in this way?

5. To learn more about how groups work together, read W. R. Bion's *Experiences in groups*. Note especially the Review at the end, entitled Group Dynamics. It is a useful summary of the conflict that often arises between cliques inside larger groups.

2
The corner-stone

What is the primary task of the church?

The work of the church falls into three categories: we worship, we express community and we witness. The chief end of man is to glorify God and to enjoy him for ever. So we worship. We worship God *together*, as a group, as a society of Christians. But the church exists as a society *within* a larger society of which the church members are also members. As a Christian society the Christians relate to each other in a spirit of sharing, of fellowship, of *koinōnia*. In the western church we have tended to allow ourselves to lose this experience of sharing, but it is still very much a reality in Asia and Africa and the Americas.

But the church exists *as* a community *in* a community, a community which has many deep needs, physical, material, mental, moral and spiritual. The church cannot really relate to this unredeemed society with *koinōnia* (as Paul expressed it in 2 Corinthians 6:14, 'what *koinōnia* has light with darkness?'), but the church does relate to the need with 'philanthropy', a concern for people; we are to do good to all men (Galatians 6:10). And there is the task of being witnesses to Christ, the evangelistic task of the church.

But which of these three tasks is the *primary* task: to

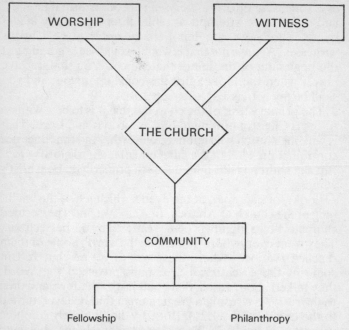

worship God, to express community or to witness to the world? Perhaps I should re-phrase the question: Why is the church left here on earth? After all, it would surely be very easy for the heavenly Fisherman, having hooked his fish, simply to land it straight into glory. It would certainly save us a great deal of trouble with prophecy and the timetable for the end-time and the rest. But God hasn't done that. And, significantly, neither has he left us here as mere individuals, but has left us as groups, as local congregations, to be *together*.

So why has God left us, as local congregations, on earth? Surely not *so that* we might worship him. We shall certainly do that very much better when we eventually get Home. Surely we are not left here *so that* we might express community, fellowship with one another and philanthropy to everyone. Our efforts at *koinōnia* are often dismal failures, and our sincere attempts at philanthropy painfully inadequate. Surely we are left here *in order to be* Christ's witnesses. At any rate that is what I would see as standing at the beginning of the life of the church: 'You shall receive power when the Holy Spirit has come upon you; and you shall be my witnesses....' (Acts 1:8).

The primary task of the church is that it is to be a witness to Jesus Christ, pointing to him as Saviour and Lord. That is why the church was left here on earth. And that does not contradict the idea of the chief end of man: to glorify God. But the church is left here on earth primarily to be Christ's witness.

Look, for example, at the events which led to the beginning of the church at Antioch. In Acts 8 we find a persecuted church, with its members being scattered by the persecution. They went everywhere 'preaching the word'. Some of them reached Antioch, where there was as yet no church. But some of these scattered Christians preached the Word; they talked about Jesus, first of all just to the Jews and then to the rest. As a result 'a great number that believed turned to the Lord' (Acts 11:21). But they didn't merely continue to exist as individuals. They started a church, they began to study, to learn, to grow. Barnabas was sent there to teach and when he arrived the church was already a going concern.

Now that is why the church is left here on earth: to be Christ's witnesses, to see people turning to the Lord and to disciple them into the church. Church Growth says: Numerical Church Growth ought to be a primary concern of the church. And this then leads on to the biblical expectation that disciples will be made who will gather into local congregations to worship their Lord and Saviour, to enjoy fellowship with other Christians and to be prepared for witness in the world.

The first principle of Church Growth
The Church Growth movement is not concerned primarily

with filling church buildings. It is concerned with the church of Jesus Christ, the world-wide family of God, concerned to see *that* church growing in numbers, growing in extent and growing in its commitment.

A moment's thought will show us that there are different kinds of growth. The total number of believers may increase. The Christians may grow spiritually, become deeper in their understanding of God's will for their lives and more fully committed to doing God's will. The church may reach out into new areas and plant new congregations. For convenience we can refer to these as *numerical* growth, *discipleship* growth and *extension* growth.

TYPES OF CHURCH GROWTH

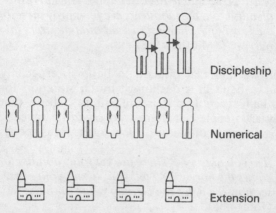

Discipleship

Numerical

Extension

The first principle of the Church Growth movement is that *numerical Church Growth ought to be a primary concern of the church*. Put it in other words: any church ought to be concerned to see people being brought to faith in Jesus Christ through its work. And the Church Growth movement would say that if this is not happening then the church ought to be trying to find out *why* it is not happening.

Now there is no suggestion here that, if only you follow the right method (*i.e.* use 'Church Growth

21

principles'), then people *will* be added to the church. It may be that all that can be done by the church is being done. It may be that no-one is standing in the way of the work of the Spirit. But Church Growth would say: ask questions, show concern, examine what is being done, pray, probe. The reason behind all this concern is the clear indication in the Bible that it *is* God's will that people should be saved. It is *not* God's will that people should be lost. And if that is the case, then we should be in a continual state of expectancy, looking for the harvest. In fact the Bible uses this very imagery to make it clear that we ought to expect numerical growth:

> 'Then Jesus said to his disciples, "The harvest is plentiful, but the labourers are few; pray therefore the Lord of the harvest to send out labourers into his harvest"' (Matthew 9:37–38).

But we find that difficult to believe, especially when we have been in a declining church situation for more than half a century. It is difficult to believe that there really are people out there who *could* be saved. Maybe at some time in the future...But again Jesus speaks to us:

> 'Do you not say, "There are yet four months, then comes the harvest"? I tell you, lift up your eyes, and see how the fields are already white for harvest' (John 4:35).

God does not want an empty heaven. Ezekiel probably expresses the mind of God most clearly:

> 'Have I any pleasure in the death of the wicked, says the Lord God, and not rather that he should turn from his way and live?' (Ezekiel 18:23);

> 'For I have no pleasure in the death of any one, says the Lord God; so turn, and live' (Ezekiel 18:32);

'Say to them, As I live, says the Lord God, I have no pleasure in the death of the wicked, but that the wicked turn from his way and live; turn back, turn back from your evil ways; for why will you die, O house of Israel?' (Ezekiel 33:11).

Paul writes to Timothy in the same style:

'... God our Saviour, who desires all men to be saved and to come to the knowledge of the truth' (1 Timothy 2:3–4).

And Peter says the same thing.

'The Lord is ... forbearing toward you, not wishing that any should perish, but that all should reach repentance' (2 Peter 3:9).

Since this is God's *will*, and since we are encouraged to look at fields which, to the ordinary Christian, appear to be very far from ready for harvesting, then surely we are wrong if we do not make harvesting a primary concern.

Not, however, as some Church Growth teachers would have it, *the* primary concern. For there are some situations which demand a very different priority. Where a congregation is split, arguing, uncaring, critical, it would be wrong to make evangelism the priority. Quite obviously our witness to what Jesus can do for the people around us must be illustrated by the evidence of the changed lives of the Christians themselves: if God can do this for me, then obviously he can do it for you. Where *my* life simply does not stand up to examination, I'd do better not to criticize *your* life!

Even here there is a danger. A good many churches are so concerned with their imperfections that they never reach a state which they feel enables them to act as witnesses. The permanent concern is with 'perfecting the saints' and, since the saints never do become perfect, nothing else ever gets on their agenda. And so the neighbours and the people at work and the young people in the youth clubs go on doing their own thing – without Christ. We must recapture the sense of urgency that is there in our task of being God's messengers, witnesses about Jesus.

Types of numerical church growth
Numerical church growth is not determined simply by counting heads on successive Sunday mornings, or even by comparing membership rolls every five years. There are churches where numbers are increasing and the ministers and congregations are a bit smug about it. But the fact that the local congregation is increasing numerically is not necessarily an indication that the church of Jesus Christ is growing. Often a successful preacher is simply skimming off dissatisfied Christians from other congregations. And so, as one church grows, another correspondingly collapses, like two balloons joined neck to neck. This kind of apparent growth is called *transfer growth*. It can be somewhat humbling to discover just where new church attenders are coming from, and especially it can be quite flattening if a visit is paid to those churches from which the new members have come.

True enough, it is sometimes just as well that these people *have* left their old churches. If the sheep are not being fed, their shepherd can hardly blame them if they sign up with another shepherd who *will* feed them. And by the same token, the new shepherd cannot be blamed for feeding them. But still it is necessary to realize, when this kind of growth is taking place, that, although numbers are increasing, this must not be taken to indicate any real penetration of the masses of the unchurched who are still out there.

Secondly, there is the situation where numbers attending the church are increasing, but new members all seem to be related to present church members: mothers and fathers, husbands and wives, brothers and sisters, and particularly children. Such growth is obviously good and something to

24

praise God for. It is especially thrilling for those whose relatives are being discipled into Christ's church. But once again it is a special kind of growth, *biological church growth*, and it does not necessarily mean that the unchurched world out there is being reached.

The fact is that our relatives stand in a special relationship to God. For example, Paul describes the non-Christian husband of a Christian wife as being 'consecrated' by his wife. And in the same passage he describes the children of Christian parents as 'holy' (1 Corinthians 7:12–16). Now Paul is careful to make it quite clear that he is not suggesting that a Christian wife somehow turns her husband and children into Christians by some kind of contagion. They are still 'unbelieving' and the Christian husband or wife has to go on living in the hope and expectation that the unbelieving partner will come to Christ. But Paul is making it clear that our unbelieving relatives *do* stand in a special relationship to God, because of our prayers for them and because of the special opportunity we have to witness to them through the very closeness of our lives together.

Biological growth, then, is a special type of growth. It involves real conversion and introduces new life, but it still leaves the world outside essentially unpenetrated.

The third type of church growth I call *evangelism growth*. In his book *Understanding Church Growth* Dr McGavran uses the words *conversion growth* to describe this category, but I am not really satisfied with that description, because *biological* growth also involves genuine conversion. But what we are both speaking about here is conversion which results from the church reaching out beyond the churched people of the community, even beyond the fringes of the church, to the unchurched millions beyond. The Church Growth movement has its particular importance right here: it makes it painfully clear to most of us that, whatever else we may be doing, we are *not* reaching out to *that* part of God's world.

I was asked to help a fairly prosperous church with a study of its outreach programme. Investigation showed that the church was effectively the only witness for Jesus Christ to something like 60,000 people. Of course these people would be able to hear the Good News on the radio or TV, but it would be so mixed up with half-truth and untruth that they would be likely to find it difficult, if not impossible, to identify the good and true and to separate it from the bad and untrue. So this church was their main hope of hearing the gospel. Visits to the church showed a very good attendance at both Sunday services, a dwindling Sunday school but a thriving young people's work. Some of the parents of the Sunday school children attended the occasional Family Services. But we estimated that over the year that church was touching, in one way or another, only some 2,000 of the 60,000 for whom it was responsible; 58,000 were left unreached. More than 96%.

When we examine the question of evangelism growth it soon becomes evident that Britain has a unique problem here, and unique structures for dealing with the problem. One of the unique structures is the Anglican system of parishes. Every house is supposed to be attached to an Anglican church, somewhere. But often this is just a nominal attachment, nominal because of the enormous numbers of *the lapsed,* people who once attended church but no longer do so, for whatever reason.

This problem of the lapsed ought to be a major preoccupation of Christians in Britain. There are enormous numbers of people who were christened into the Anglican church, but who have never gone any further. In 1979 it was computed that there were 26.8 million people born and resident in England who had been baptized in the Anglican church. Of these fewer than ten million had got as far as confirmation. And on Christmas Day, when most Anglicans would make a special effort to take communion, there were less than two million communicants. Twenty-five million, almost half the population of the UK, must be included in the total of the lapsed. Then there are the people for whom there are no statistics at all, the hundreds of thousands who once attended Sunday school but now never go near a

26

DEGREES OF COMMITMENT:
THE ANGLICAN CHURCH IN ENGLAND 1979
Figures from the Statistical Office of the Church of England, London

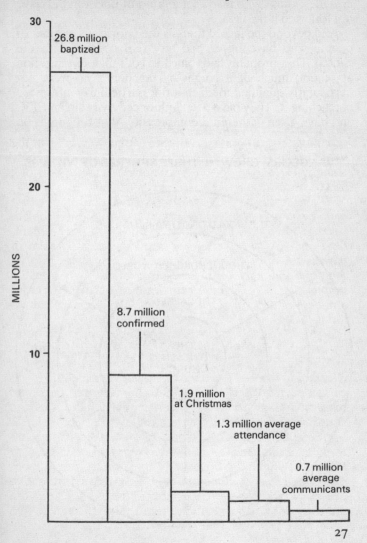

26.8 million baptized

8.7 million confirmed

1.9 million at Christmas

1.3 million average attendance

0.7 million average communicants

MILLIONS

church. These, too, are part of the army of the lapsed. To these must be added the drop-outs from the evangelistic crusades, those who made some kind of decision but have not followed it through.

And beyond the lapsed there is the enormous number of people who have never had any real contact with the church. They probably had some kind of religious education at school, much of it taught by teachers who were not particularly qualified to teach it nor particularly interested in teaching it. They have been influenced by radio and TV, and have often gathered the impression that religion is on

EVANGELISM GROWTH: THREE SPHERES OF WITNESS

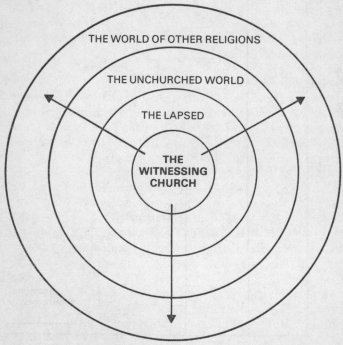

THE WORLD OF OTHER RELIGIONS

THE UNCHURCHED WORLD

THE LAPSED

THE
WITNESSING
CHURCH

the way out, that the Bible has been shown to be of anti-quarian interest only and that modern man can no longer seriously believe in God. Evangelism growth has to take seriously the problem of how to reach these people with the Good News.

But there is still one more circle of people to be reached: the adherents of other religions. To the comparative hand-ful of people born and bred in Britain who have become Muslims and Hindus, there must now be added the flood of immigrants. In 1980 there were already some 800,000 Muslims in Britain. Where once we could pass on the responsibility for sharing the Good News with Muslims to our overseas missionaries, we must now consider the challenge here at home, on our own doorstep.

Evangelism growth is, perhaps, the principal challenge that the Church Growth movement brings to the churches today. Church Growth thinking makes it painfully clear to us that we are not doing very well in this area of our responsibility.

Discipleship growth

Although Church Growth does emphasize *numerical* growth, it obviously also recognizes the importance of other types of growth. But there must be no mistaking the fact that Church Growth insists on the priority of *numerical* growth. The Church *ought* to be primarily concerned to see that men and women are being brought to Christ.

Discipleship growth is the kind of growth expected of every Christian. The Bible uses two particular illustrations of this kind of growth: the picture of a baby growing, changing from a diet of milk to an eventual diet of 'strong meat' or 'solid food' (Hebrews 5:11–14), and the picture of a tree growing upwards by pushing its roots downwards (Colossians 2:7).

The Bible realistically expects the young Christian to take 'milk' in the early days: simple teaching, basic concepts. But the Bible also expects that this situation will not continue indefinitely: the child must grow and take solid food, the Christian must mature and develop in discipleship. But what is milk and what is meat? Here we can easily get things wrong and assume that solid food means the study of prophecy, while milk means the basics of Christian behaviour. The Bible takes a different view.

The writer to the Hebrews defines the elementary things as repentance, faith, baptism, ordination, resurrection and the last judgment (Hebrews 6:1–2). Theologians have impressively labelled these doctrines soteriology, ecclesiology and eschatology, but the Epistle to the Hebrews puts them into the category of elementary doctrines. The writer urges us to go on from there. The people to whom the letter was first written had *not* gone on from there. The basic teaching ought to have led them on to a deeper level of Christian life. They ought to have been producing 'vegetation' useful to those for whose sake they were being 'cultivated'; they were to produce the kind of lives which would meet the needs of the people among whom they lived and witnessed. The basic doctrines are not given as an end in themselves, as though more careful and thorough and precise definitions and theories were the goal in mind. Not at all. The goal in mind when we study doctrine is the purifying of our lives. 'If God is like this, then what kind of a person ought I to be?' 'If the cross accomplishes this, why then should I still be caught up in habitual sin?' Doctrine is basic. Nevertheless more doctrine does not necessarily indicate maturity. *That* is seen in the quality of my life.

Frankly, it is rather simple to master the basic doctrines of the Christian faith. What is really difficult is to *live* God's way. And *that* means discipleship growth.

Paul refers to discipleship growth in Colossians 1:28–29. We proclaim Christ, he says,

> '... *warning every man and teaching every man in all wisdom, that we may present every man mature in Christ. For this I toil, striving with all the energy which he mightily inspires within me.*'

Paul wanted to see every Christian growing up, becoming mature. He did not merely have a vague, pious hope that somehow it would happen. He had the kind of deep concern that a father might well have for his children. No father wants his children to remain babies. Paul urgently wanted to see growth in his spiritual children. Note the extraordinary concentration in Paul's words of 'power' concepts: I *toil, striving* with all the *energy* which God *mightily* inspires within me.

The Christian Education programme

But *how* are young Christians to grow? One of the great lacks in most British churches is any kind of serious Christian Education programme. In fact many ministers do not even know what a Christian Education programme is. If you look at the usual kind of teaching programme in the average church, it really does seem rather odd. I don't know of any other place where education is given quite in this way. We put all the Christians into the church on Sunday, natural ages from fifteen to ninety or so, spiritual ages from new-born babes to nonagenarians, and teach them all together. It doesn't make any difference whether they are young or old, single or married, men or women, university lecturers or barely able to read: all learn together. The preacher cannot give them milk, because most are beyond that stage; neither can he give them solid food, because a good many are not able to digest it. So he spreads out the usual breadcrumbs and hopes that, somehow, his congregation will be satisfied. Or, to be brutally frank, he probably doesn't give that much thought to what he is doing.

A Christian Education programme implies that each Christian receives an education that is appropriate to his particular stage of development. There are separate programmes for children, for adolescents, for young marrieds, for what I call the 'middlies' and for older Christians. Obviously this means that the church membership is divided up for the teaching sessions, just as children in school are divided up and for the same reason. Education is essentially cumulative: what is taught today is built on what was learnt yesterday. And what is learnt today is related to today's needs.

The process is not quite as simple as it sounds, because every Christian has two ages; his natural age and his spiritual age. Both ages indicate something of his educational needs, but neither can be used as an automatic guide to those needs. A new convert to Christ may already know all the basic doctrines, especially if he comes from the first sphere of evangelism, the sphere of the lapsed. A person may have been a Christian for many years and yet may never have had the basic teachings explained intelligibly to him. In fact, as a church's Christian Education programme develops, the situation will gradually become much simpler as new Christians are systematically taken into 'nursery' groups, or whatever they are called, and as the older Christians catch up on all that they have missed.

When Christians are all expected to learn together in the traditional 'mid-week meeting', the diet they get is unsatisfactory. For some it is too rich, while for others it is too thin and they are left like theological Oliver Twists still asking for more. Discipleship Growth seems to depend on some kind of Christian Education programme to ensure that the right diet is found for everyone. There are suggestions for starting such a programme on pages 105-107.

Extension growth

The third kind of growth involves outreach into new areas. It is the kind of work that missionary societies were created for, and also the kind of work at which C. H. Spurgeon excelled. He trained ministers in his Pastors' College and then sent them all over London, over to the Continent and even to Australia, to plant new churches.

The Great Commission to make disciples of all nations (Matthew 28:19–20) has never been rescinded. We are still responsible to go into all the world; and, of course, the churches in the rest of the world are equally responsible to go into all the world. All churches at all times and in every part of the world have the responsibility for reaching out, for extension growth.

The objection is sometimes made that there are already churches in every part of Britain. As we have seen, every house in Britain falls in some parish, but that does not mean that everyone is, in fact, being offered the Good News. Nor is it true that because there is a church *building* there is necessarily a *church*. New churches *are* still needed, and I would want to go further and say that where existing 'churches' are not witnessing for Jesus nor sharing the Good News, then a new church ought to be planted.

Sometimes, of course, it is possible to move live Christians into dead churches and thereby bring about a resurrection.

But missionary work – and extension growth, whether it means planting a new church in Birmingham or in Buenos Aires, *is* missionary work – is hard work. It is much more comfortable to stay at home and continue to enjoy all the comforts of the home church, with the established congregation and the reliable central heating and the experienced leadership. It is difficult for Christians who belong to a successful church with a couple of hundred members to contemplate leaving all this to go just a couple of miles away to plant a new church on a housing estate, where for a good many years it is going to mean meeting in the local school hall. And yet people who find such a commitment difficult or even impossible will still applaud missionaries who travel a couple of thousand miles to plant new churches at considerably more inconvenience than they are likely to experience.

The Church Growth movement challenges churches to take seriously every aspect of growth. Numerical growth: seeing men and women discipled to Christ. Discipleship growth: seeing Christians learning what their faith is all about and living transformed lives because of it, lives that glorify God and are a real challenge to the unredeemed world around them. Extension growth: the readiness to abandon the comfort of the familiar for new endeavours, new areas, to present Jesus Christ where he has not previously been known.

No methodology is going to be offered to us that will guarantee full churches, but a call to look more closely at all that we are doing to see if our primary task is being performed, to see if we are really doing the job for which God has left us here on earth.

But our trouble is that we don't really expect people to become Christians. T.W. Medhurst was the first student to be accepted for training by Spurgeon. After he had been preaching for some three months he came to Spurgeon thoroughly discouraged: not one person, so far as he knew, had been converted through his preaching. Spurgeon looked at him ponderously. Then he asked:

'Do you expect the Lord to save souls every time *you* open your mouth?'

'Oh, no, sir!'

'Then that's just the reason why you've not had conversions.'

NOW WHAT DO WE DO?

1. Statistics

What statistics have you got for your church? Attendance figures? Maybe over a good many years? (If not, now is the time to start!) Maybe numbers attending Easter Communion? Or older church members may be able to give some useful estimates. Figures for the church offerings? You will need to do something about allowing for inflation before you can really start to compare these figures, though. For example, if 1980 had a 20% rate of inflation, you would need to reduce the 1980 total collections by a fifth before this figure could meaningfully be compared with the 1979 figure.

a. What are the apparent trends?

Rapid — Slight — Static — Growing — Growing
decline   decline   slightly   rapidly

b. How does this compare with the growth of the local population? (You can usually get relevant figures from the local Council.)

Rapid __ Slight __ Static __ Growing __ Growing
decline   decline   slightly   rapidly

c. Compare the results of a. and b. Does anything significant appear from these estimates? Write down a single sentence which summarizes what you conclude from these figures, even if you have to write the one word 'Nothing'.

2. Newcomers
Either look over your church records or else take a regular check over the next six months to see where new folks are coming from.

a. How many newcomers came to church in the last six months?
b. Where have they come from? Why did they come?
   Visitors, just passing through?
   Transfers from another church?
   Relatives of present regulars?
   Outsiders?
c. Find out what brought each one into your church.

3. Losses
What about the loss of church-goers? Find out how many people have stopped attending the church over the past year.

a. How many have stopped coming?
b. Find out why they have stopped coming:
   death, illness, age?
   moved away?
   didn't like the church?
   a disagreement?
c. Where are they now?
d. What is being done to stay in touch with them?

4. Outreach

What is the church's programme to reach the following people:

a. Parents of Sunday School children, of members of the youth organizations and of the young people generally?

b. People who have been baptized, confirmed, sung in the choir?

c. Drop-outs from Sunday School or the youth organizations?

d. Senior citizens and the infirm in general?

e. School children? Is the minister involved at all in local school assemblies or RE classes? Is there any support for the Inter-School Christian Fellowship? Are there contacts with local school Christian Unions?

f. Immigrants? Is there any attempt to offer help in settling in? Any English classes?

g. Students? Does the church advertise on local college notice-boards? Is help offered with finding lodgings? Are there special lectures for students? Are homes open for hospitality at the weekend?

h. And what about the people who never go to any church? The people who religiously wash their cars on Sunday and that's all the religion they seem to have. The people who don't even *want* any 'religion'. Somehow they ought to be given the chance to hear. But how?

Any obvious blanks here? Maybe a sub-group (about five members) could look at the results of this survey and suggest improvements to the church's strategy for reaching these different groups.

5. Extension growth

Is there, somewhere near the church, a district that doesn't *have* a church yet? Should we start one? Could we start one? How could we start one?

6. Something to read

You might start with Robin Thomson's book, *Can British churches grow?* Unit 3 deals with statistics of church growth. You will need to make up your own mind about the real value for your church of spending time on certain detailed surveys (would you expect to learn anything that you couldn't learn more simply by a quick look around the church on Sunday evening?).

And you might like to look at David Sheppard's *Built as a city*. This is a serious and sometimes heavy-going study of the city-church. But some parts are of real importance: chapter 2 (pages 36-47), 'Church life in the city', and especially chapter 8, 'The church's task', which emphasizes the value of local leadership because of the local man's knowledge of local conditions.

7. Starting a Christian Education programme

a. It is easy to make a beginning. Have you got a Track One, Step One, Base-line, call-it-what-you-will class for new Christians? If not, start one. Decide on what you are going to teach. You will need to answer some pretty basic questions, such as: Who is Jesus? Can a Christian still...? Why should I pray? What is the best way to read the Bible? The series of books published by Kingsway will help here: 'I want to know what the Bible teaches about...'.

Don't just announce the course. Put a sign-up sheet on the notice-board, but make sure before you do so that you have three or more people all ready to sign up. Then potential signers are not faced with a depressingly blank sheet.

b. The rest of your programme will depend on the size of your church. You should plan *two* main lines of classes: (i) A continuation of the Track One or whatever nursery class in basic Christian teaching. The list of topics is enormous, but *make a list,* otherwise the church will just get a diet of subjects that someone happens to like talking about. (ii) Classes for different social needs: for young people at school, for young marrieds, and so on. (See also pages 104-107, below.)

The secret of success is twofold: (i) You must be answering questions that people are actually asking.

(ii) You must get people to opt in by signing up for a class, rather than opting out by simply not turning up.

c. Don't worry if some teaching is done outside the church, in evening classes or even by correspondence courses.

d. If at all possible appoint someone to be 'Director of Education'. No, of course you don't *have* to call him that, but someone ought to keep an eye on everyone to see that they are all being fed. See Colossians 1:28–29 for a reminder of the urgency here.

3
Full employment

In many of the more traditional churches the work of the church has been the responsibility either of the minister exclusively or, at best, of the minister plus his select group of assistants. The remainder of the church feels that it has done its part of the task when it has paid all the bills and attended the various functions that make up the church's weekly programme. The church is allowed to become 'his church', or 'their church', which is attended by the rest of the congregation. It is not '*our* church'. Sometimes this covert assumption becomes painfully explicit.

I recall one church which had for many years employed a full-time caretaker. But the time came when he had to retire and for several months there was no-one to clean the church or the various halls and rooms. So at one morning service the minister asked for volunteers to turn out on the following Thursday evening to clean the church. After the service one of the church members was overheard telling another: 'It's his church... let *him* clean it'!

The one-man ministry effectively accomplishes two things: it kills off the one man and it paralyses the rest. In fact, if the situation is allowed to go on long enough, the congregation may not be merely paralysed: it may become petrified, incapable of being reanimated. Some ministers have been so effective in imposing the idea of the one-man ministry that, despite honest attempts to rectify the situation, it has proved impossible to get the congregation moving again.

Within any church the Holy Spirit is at work *actively,* but there is a further *potentiality* of the Spirit, determined by the gifting of church members. That is to say, the Spirit distributes gifts to the Christians and he is then *potentially* able to work through those gifts. But the Holy Spirit cannot turn them into his dynamic until the gifts are *used.* It is like a gardener who hands out spades, forks, rakes and hoes to an assortment of people because he has a great deal of work to do in his garden. He has the tools and he has the people, and so *potentially* there is work for all to get on with. But he cannot do anything if the people simply sit down on the lawn and have a picnic. And that is not an unfair picture of the situation in many a church: one man wielding spade, fork, hoe and lawn-mower, but never able to get round all the garden, while the dozens sit and watch him doing it, now admiring him for his expertise and now criticizing him for the unpruned roses or the poor crop of potatoes.

The concept of gifting

What *are* spiritual gifts? In 1 Corinthians 12–14 Paul deals with them in some detail; they are described as 'manifestations of the Spirit':

> '*To each is given the manifestation of the Spirit for the common good*' (1 Corinthians 12:7).

That is to say, spiritual gifts are special abilities given to Christians which enable the Spirit to 'manifest' or 'show' himself, to show that he is there and at work. In the same passage Paul goes on to give some examples of these gifts.

He mentions 'the utterance of wisdom', 'the gift of wise speech' (NEB), and he differentiates between that and 'the utterance of knowledge', which NEB helpfully paraphrases, 'another, by the power of the same Spirit, can put the deepest knowledge into words'. Paul is here differentiating between *sophia*, the kind of wisdom that sheer experience might bring to a man, and *gnōsis*, which is more the kind of knowledge that may be learnt. Paul insists, however, that the *spiritual* gift of being wise, or of having knowledge, is superhuman; it must not be confused with mere natural ability. Spiritual grey-matter does not necessarily come with grey hair; it is sovereignly given by the Spirit.

He mentions the gift of special faith. Although all Christians have faith, some have special gifting in that area. When some new outreach is being planned these are the people who can assure the rest that it is going to be all right; when a new building is being built these are the people who are certain that the money will all come in. And, of course, their faith is a tremendous encouragement to the rest.

There is the spiritual gift of healing, and it is interesting to note here that Paul suggests that to a particular individual the Spirit might give *gifts* of healing; not the power to heal whom he will, but individual gifts of healing, given in specific situations, it would seem, to heal particular people. In a more general way he speaks of the ability to 'work miracles', and presumably that might also include the ability to heal. He mentions the gift of prophecy, 'the gift of speaking God's message' (GNB), and he has a good deal more to say about this in chapter 14.

The last three gifts are clearly related to one another: first, the ability to distinguish between spirits, to distinguish between words which come from God through his Holy Spirit and through his messengers, and words which might purport to come from God but which are designed to mislead the church and come from Satan and his messengers. Then there is the gift of speaking in tongues, which was a confusing phenomenon then as it still is today, since it is common to most religions. Adherents of the pagan religions sometimes spoke in tongues; Muslim mystics speak in tongues and so do the 'wise men' of African traditional religion. And so this gift is carefully sandwiched

41

between the gift of distinguishing spirits and the gift of being able to interpret the tongues, the unknown languages.

In this passage it is easy to identify *nine* spiritual gifts, and further on in the chapter other gifts are indicated, including the gift of being able to help others (verse 28) and the gift of administration.

There is another reference to spiritual gifts in Ephesians 4:11–12:

> '*And his gifts were that some should be apostles, some prophets, some evangelists, some pastors and teachers, to equip the saints for the work of ministry, for building up the body of Christ.*'

Notice that in each passage there is emphasis on the purpose of the gifting: that the Holy Spirit should be able to get on with his twofold work of bringing unbelievers under conviction and of leading the believers on to maturity. The gifts are not intended merely to enable us to play parlour tricks, to impress our friends or to provide us with some kind of ego-trip.

Notice, however, that there is no suggestion that these lists of spiritual gifts are exhaustive and that there are no other gifts. I should have supposed that singing was a spiritual gift, as well as the ability to lead others in singing, and that counselling was a spiritual gift, and hospitality. In modern times we might think of special gifts given to Sunday School teachers or Boys' Brigade officers. And what about those practical gifts that have so enriched some churches: gifts of carpentry, painting and gardening?

The gifts of the Spirit and the work of the church

These spiritual gifts are given to Christians by the Holy Spirit as he wishes (1 Corinthians 12:11). The New Testament assumes that Christians are part of some local congregation. So then it would seem right to assume that the pattern of gifts distributed to the members of any particular congregation is related to the work which the

Holy Spirit wants done in that congregation and by that congregation. But if the local church is a one-man operation, there is no situation in which the church members can use their gifts. The work of the Spirit cannot be effected. The spades and hoes and rakes are there, but they are not being used.

The second principle of the Church Growth movement is that the church should activate all its members. Only in that way can the whole rainbow-spread of the Spirit's activity be made possible. Only in that way can we avoid quenching the Spirit.

But when we examine what the churches are actually doing, we find that their programmes are determined *historically*. 'We have always had a Boys' Brigade company. True enough, the original officers have all long since left the church, but we feel that we must keep the company going. Unfortunately we don't seem to have the right kind of leadership for this kind of work. On the other hand there's George....' Yes, there's the ever-willing George, always to be relied on. He knows that it is not really his cup of tea, but rather than see the work come to a halt.... So the company struggles on for a few more years and George has a pretty thin time of it. But would it not seem right that, *if* the Spirit wanted the Boys' Brigade company to carry on, he would provide the leadership gifts for it? And conversely, if he does not provide the leadership for it, might it not be because the company does not form part of his plans for this church?

It is important for us to realize that the church, the local congregation, is not a static but a dynamic body. The membership is continually changing. Former members change their jobs and move away from the district. They retire. They die. New members move in. There are conversions. And so the pattern of gifts in the church is always changing, too. Church Growth thinking would suggest that the programme of any church should be related to the pattern of gifting in the church *now* and not merely to the pattern inherited from some past congregation which was differently gifted. And this in turn would suggest that the leadership of the church should be continually observing the church's pattern of gifting as church members come and go, in order to identify new gifts acquired and old gifts lost.

But there is more to it than that. The leadership of the church should be aware of the gifts of the church members, but should also be concerned to see that where necessary the right kind of training is given, so that the gifts are maximized. Preachers need training; teachers need to get some formal grounding in theology. The minister may be able to train such people himself; the church might have to consider sending one of its members to a theological college.

Identifying the gifts in the church

The actual range of spiritual gifts in a church may not be recognized where a minister is determined not to look for them, or is not even aware that they might be there. A Baptist minister in Surrey had regularly led and taught the mid-week prayer and Bible study session at his church right through all the years of his ministry, but only thirty or so of his 200-plus membership turned up. It occurred to him one day that there really must be others in his church capable of teaching.

So he put up a notice on the church notice-board, inviting church members to share in the Wednesday night teaching programme. Four of his members accepted the invitation, offering an assortment of subjects including church history. He accepted all four offers and devised a new form of Wednesday evening programme. The church came together, sang and prayed, and then divided up into four groups. Everyone opted *in* to whichever group appealed, where previously their only recourse was to opt *out* by not turning up. The result has been more than 150 meeting on Wednesday evenings. The gifts were there, and when the gifts were used then the Holy Spirit was set free to do the work he had wanted to do all along.

But we ought not to restrict our ideas of spiritual gifting to such obvious gifts as teaching and preaching. Paul seems

44

to suggest that the Spirit has spiritual gifts for every Christian:

> '*All these are inspired by one and the same Spirit, who apportions* to each one *individually as he wills*' (1 Corinthians 12:11).

The church, then, should be concerned to identify all the gifts and to structure its programme so that they can all be used. So how can the church go about this particular task?

One rather simple way is for the church leaders to produce a list of gifts: I would include everything from preaching and healing to leading the singing and arranging the flowers, from typing the church bulletin to caring for the church gardens. A very long list, with space beside each gift sufficient to allow for the writing of a couple of names. Then (perhaps at a church away-day) everyone is given a copy of the list and invited to put his or her name beside any gift that he might feel God has given to him.

True enough, that could promote pride, but Scripture *does* encourage us to assess ourselves:

> '*I bid every one among you not to think of himself more highly than he ought to think, but to think with sober judgement, each according to the measure of faith which God has assigned him*' (Romans 12:3).

Now this verse occurs precisely in the context of the work of the local church, which is described as resembling a body. The implication seems to be that each part of the body should be aware of its own function: am I an ear, or a tongue, or a foot, or what? Because only when I know what I am can I get on with my task. It is ludicrously possible for an ear to develop a crushing inferiority complex because it is doing its best to be a tongue.

In the same passage Paul goes right on to encourage Christians to get on with their work in accordance with their spiritual gifts:

45

'So we are to use our different gifts in accordance with the grace that God has given us. If our gift is to speak God's message, we should do it according to the faith that we have; if it is to serve, we should serve; if it is to teach, we should teach; if it is to encourage others, we should do so' (Romans 12:6–8, GNB).

Obviously, if we are to use our gifts, we shall need to know what they are. But we must face up to the real difficulty which is produced by people who think that they have gifts which, in fact, they have not got at all, while others do have certain gifts although they have never realized it.

This is where the church comes in. As we have already seen, lists of potential spiritual gifts can be produced and distributed to each person who prayerfully indicates on his list which of the gifts he feels that he has, using, of course, the 'sober judgment' of Romans 12:3. But now the process is repeated. New lists are distributed to each person, but this time the aim is to have each person write down beside each spiritual gift the names of people in the church whom they feel have been given that gift. Then it is the task of the church leaders to compare the lists, to see how far the church concurs with the individual's assessment of his own gifts.

It is quite remarkable to see how in such a simple exercise the Holy Spirit can make plain to the church what gifts he has distributed to the members of the congregation, how these gifts relate to what the Holy Spirit wants done in the church, which gifts are already recognized and being used and which gifts have been so far unused because they have not been recognized. The identification of new and hitherto unrecognized gifts in the congregation may well solve the perennial problem of churches, the problem posed by too few people doing too many things. Church leaders often genuinely feel that there is simply no-one else in the church who is capable of doing the jobs they are doing. But it surely cannot be God's will to have the handful rushing about like bureaucratic Marthas, often nursing an unexpressed grudge against the very Marys they have themselves immobilized?

To make the over-all picture even more confusing, it is by no means always clear just how much work is being done by some people. The position of the Baptist deacon, for example, does not involve him in one job but in many. He attends the deacons' meetings. He helps with visiting those who are unwell. He is at the church door on Sundays to welcome visitors. He represents the church at occasional conferences. He may have to take a turn at acting as caretaker. He may be given responsibility for looking after church repairs, or keeping the church accounts, or contacting visiting preachers.

THE SELF-LIMITING CONGREGATION

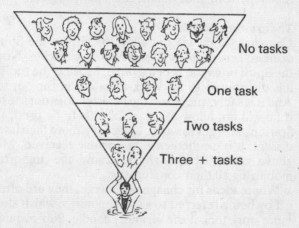

No tasks

One task

Two tasks

Three + tasks

The level of loading

A useful exercise for the church is to survey its members to find out just how the total load of work is distributed in the church: how many people have one job, how many have two, three and so on. Care needs to be taken that the concept of *a job* is carefully defined: as we have seen, the position of deacon would involve not one but several jobs.

Where surveys of this kind are carried out it is usually found that the resulting profile is a kind of inverted pyramid, the one minister, with a multitude of tasks, groaning at the bottom, and the vast majority of the church in the smiling ranks at the top with nothing to do except to pay and maybe to pray.

Perversely it is often the people at the bottom of the pile, the frantically scrabbling workaholics, who are the most reluctant to see things change. Few ministers are prepared to settle seriously to the task of training someone else to do their work. In the short term (and that is an important qualification) it is so much easier and so much more satisfying to do it yourself. Such an attitude kills off the minister and the church is left without a trained leadership in the interim period before they find another candidate for a repeat performance of the same killing regime.

The growing church

Churches which will not allow the gifts of the Spirit to be exercised are necessarily self-limiting churches. Not all that the Spirit *might* do is being done, because the tools that he has distributed to his work-force are never put to work. And it is sadly true that if the minister does not see this, and if he will not allow the spiritual gifts to be used, then the Spirit *cannot* get to work. Unbelief is more than intellectual dissent: it is disobedience to teaching received. Ministers, above all others, *ought* to know the importance of mobilizing all their congregation.

Where ideas for change do emerge, they are often killed off by being referred to a sub-committee which already has more work than it can seriously handle. Sub-committees of non-growing churches are often overloaded with work, and since there are too few people to go round, the committees themselves guarantee that the church's ministry will not develop. It develops until the handful of activists is fully employed, and steadfastly resists any further growth. A church will grow best when it is structured for growth.

The structures suited to a church of twenty are quite

different from the structures needed for a church of two hundred. It is not merely a question of adding more elders or deacons or of expanding the Parochial Church Council. *New* structures are needed, a new type of leadership is demanded.

In his book *The practice of management,* Peter Drucker comments: 'At its inception a company is often the lengthened shadow of one man. But it will not grow and survive unless the one-man top is converted into a team.' That is true not only of companies but also of many churches. Men of vision and fine preachers get them going, sometimes after years of stagnation. But unless the one man is turned into a team the prognosis is certain: a man... a movement... a monument.

In a growing church new problems arise and there are new needs. A new style of 'management' becomes necessary. No one person can hope to meet all the pastoral needs of young and old, marrieds and singles, men and women, educated and not-so-educated, housewives, actors. carpenters and the rest. But as the church grows, so the number of gifts in the church grows and the pattern of gifting changes. Church Growth thinking counsels: mobilize all your resources.

NOW WHAT DO WE DO?

Is it time for a church away-day? Say from 11 until 4 on a Saturday. Can you get another church to help by providing a team to arrange a separate pro- gramme for the children? (Otherwise several of your really active members will be off caring for the children instead of contributing to the discussion.) Do not overload the programme with discussions and talks. Have plenty of time for singing and simply sitting around chatting. A pot-luck lunch is good, much better than everyone bringing his own sand- wiches. Try to get some of the following fitted in during the day.

1. Skills in the church

Duplicate a list of skills which are needed – or which might be needed in the church. Leave a space beside each of these skills, large enough to make it possible for a name to be written in. Here is the kind of list I mean:

Art work (posters, notice-boards, *etc.*)	_____
Audio-visuals (show slides, films)	_____
Bible teaching	_____
Bookstall	_____
Business administration	_____
Carpentry	_____
Cooking	_____
Driving (collect people)	_____
Evangelism	_____
Financial matters	_____
Gardening	_____
Hospitality	_____
House-to-house visits	_____
Leading discussion groups	_____
Men's work	_____
Music: instrumental	_____
leading singing	_____
singing	_____
Open-air work	_____
Photography	_____
Prayer	_____
Preaching	_____
Reading in public	_____
Secretarial: typing	_____
correspondence	_____
Song leader (see under music)	
Sunday school: organizer	_____
teacher	_____
Transport (organize rotas)	_____
Ushering	_____
Vehicle maintenance (parish 'bus)	_____

Visiting (pastoral)	_____
Women's work	_____
Writing articles (for local press)	_____
Young people's work	_____

a. Hand out the lists, and ask everyone to put his name on the paper and then tick any of the skills he thinks that he has. Make sure that everyone understands the teaching of chapter 3 about the rightness of Christians sensibly assessing their abilities.

b. After those sheets have been collected, hand out fresh lists and ask everyone to fill in the names of people from the church who they think have the gifts listed. Just one or perhaps two names against each skill.

c. Collect those sheets as well. Later on a group from the church should compare the two sets.

Any surprises? Are the identified gifts being employed? Is the programme of the church clearly related to the skills available? What changes are to be taken as a result of using this questionnaire?

2. The work to be done

Give everyone a blank piece of paper. Ask them to write down each job they do regularly in connection with the church. 'Deacon' or 'churchwarden' is a position, not a job. Putting out chairs for the Sunday school, calling for Mrs Johnson, counting the collection, making the tea at the women's meeting...these are all jobs.

Collect the papers (they can be unsigned if your folks prefer to be anonymous).

a. What is the total weekly work-load of the church?

b. How many people in the church have no regular task at all?

c. How many have only one regular task? Two? and so on.

Is this distribution satisfactory? Take into consideration the home responsibilities carried by parents, for example. Are some people overloaded? What

51

changes should be made? Can the list of skills from the earlier exercise be put to use now?

3. Something to read
Unit 8 of Robin Thomson's *Can British churches grow?* is entitled 'How do we get moving and who does it?'. A lot of helpful suggestions will be found there. But when people *do* start to work together a lot of friction can develop. The closer the contact the worse the friction. A strong recommendation, therefore, of Derek and Nancy Copley's *Building with bananas*. When I first saw the book I assumed that it was either another trendy book on missions or else something on third-world hunger. It isn't. People, say the Copleys, are supposed to be like bricks, a suitable shape for building into a church, but in fact they are more like bananas, a most unsuitable shape for the purposes of building. Humorous, but *very* practical for the church that is seriously planning to work as a community. Note especially chapter 6, 'Seeing other people's viewpoint'. What about question 4 at the end of the chapter: 'To what extent do you consider that much of your thinking is strongly influenced by your past?' And try chapter 7, 'Women in the church', which opens up a whole area of discussion that is scarcely touched on in my chapter.

4. For discussion
What produces 'one-man-band' churches? Try it this way. Arrange an evening meeting and have the church members explain why a minister would hesitate to delegate too much of his work. Then have the minister explain why the congregation might hesitate to do much of his work. And the crunch question: what can we do to spread the load, to set the minister free to do what he is best at and to put the congregation to work so that they can grow, too?

5. Be specific
a. Could we do anything to improve the music in the church? Could we use more musical instruments? What about choirs? A men's choir? Soloists? Does

our singing need someone to lead it? Does our singing drag? New hymns? A new hymn book? *Psalm Praise*? *Sound of Living Waters*?

b. Do some folks need some training to develop their gifts? Preaching? Counselling? Singing?

c. Where might we make a start? At what point could we bring someone into the work of the church without causing too much fuss? For the reading of the Bible on Sunday? Has someone a real gift for leading a congregation in prayer?

4

Responsive people

From time to time the Holy Spirit begins to move whole classes of people – age groups, families, even entire villages – into repentance and faith. The immediate cause of the movement to God may be an individual, like Billy Graham, perhaps, or it may be some catastrophic event, such as a famine. But behind the immediate cause is the Holy Spirit.

It is one of the principles of the Church Growth movement that *the church should concentrate its resources on responsive elements of society.* In other words, if the Holy Spirit begins to move a group of people to repentance and faith, then the church is responsible to move in with its available resources.

Before illustrating this principle, one misunderstanding must be cleared up: this principle does *not* mean that Christian witness should be abandoned where there is no apparent response. The principle has sometimes been interpreted in that way, but such an attitude would be unbiblical: we are always to 'go into all the world'. God will always be calling people to work in places where nothing seems to happen. Sowing *may* take place a very long time before the harvest begins to appear. In particular, this principle does not mean that the Christian church should abandon mission to Islam. What we *may* need to do, still following Church Growth ideas, is to examine the way in which mission to Islam is being carried on.

This opens the way for the illustration of the principle. Here are two illustrations, both from Ethiopia and both involving Islam. The first shows the far-reaching consequences of ignoring the principle.

Muhammad was born in Mecca in AD 570. His teaching at first was directed primarily against the polytheism of his day, against the obvious exploitation of 'god' by the entrepreneurs of Mecca. Every clan had its deity, and more than 300 idol representations of the gods of Arabia were housed in the Kaaba in Mecca. The annual pilgrimages to the Kaaba brought in a very satisfactory revenue to the rulers of the city and the traders who operated there. Muhammad spoke out against all this, against the absurdity of the hundreds of gods and the evil of the exploitation of the pilgrims. Not surprisingly his teaching was resisted and resented. Persecution developed. His followers were illtreated.

At last, in AD 615, he encouraged about a hundred of his followers to flee to Ethiopia, just across the Red Sea. There they were well received by the king. The rulers of Mecca demanded that the refugees be returned to Mecca, but the king refused to give them up. And it was just there that the very first 'conversions' from Muhammand's way, Islam, to Christianity took place. The fact is that Muhammad had only a very inaccurate, imprecise idea of what Christianity believed: he had presented it to his followers as a kind of tri-theism. The refugees heard the Good News and some were converted. Some eventually returned to Arabia. One of the converts is reported to have told Muhammad's companions: 'We now see clearly, but you are still blinking'!

But here is the point. It did not occur to the church in Ethiopia to send teachers to Mecca in order to correct the ideas of Muhammad. Even at that stage in the development of his teaching it might have been possible to turn him back from what was to become a head-on collison with

Christianity (SS). Islam might well have become a badly-needed reform movement within Arabian Christianity. But the Ethiopian church has never been a missionary church. No-one went. The result: Islam.

That was more than 1,000 years ago. Now for the second illustration of the principle, from more recent times. At the end of the last century a certain sheikh, living in the north of Ethiopia, became a Christian through reading an Arabic New Testament. The conversion of Sheikh Zacharyas led to the conversion of other Muslims, and reports speak of 5,000 turning to Christ. He was given a personal letter from the Emperor, authorizing him to preach.

In the 1920s, the successor to Zacharyas, a man named Yussuf, contacted the Sudan Interior Mission, asking for help for the converts. They needed literature and a teacher. But it was the time of the American Depression, the SIM work in Ethiopia had scarcely begun and missionaries were simply not available. Some Christian literature was sent, but that was all. In late 1934 Dr Lambie, then the SIM's Field Director in Ethiopia, was able to visit Sokota, where this great movement had been taking place. He was too late. Yussuf was dead, ambushed and shot. Leadership of the Christians had passd to the Governor of the town, an old man who was now blind. The believers were a mere handful. And with the Italian invasion of Ethiopia at hand, the opportunity in the north was already gone. Today nothing remains of that movement.

The third principle of Church Growth suggests that where such movements occur, the church should strain every nerve in order to move in to meet the challenge, to take the opportunity. This would suggest that a local church has the responsibility to be aware of the existence of responsive groups, and then to move in to meet the need.

Responsive groups today
But are there, in fact, groups of people, in Britain for example, who are responsive to the Good News today? The answer is an unqualified Yes!

56

In the 1970s and 1980s a new pattern of church attendance has been emerging: a strange pattern, that demands some explanation. In church after church we find a large number of people aged fifty or more, and we are now finding large numbers of young people, aged from fifteen to twenty-five. But in between...nothing, or very few. Here is an explanation.

During the Second World War very large numbers of men were thrown together, often with long hours with nothing to do, except talk. Of course, in between times there were periods of frenetic activity. But in the periods of inactivity they talked and planned. Especially they talked about the new Britain that they were determined to bring in after the war. They had seen privilege at its worst and they had seen religion at its most perverted. Apart from a few honourable exceptions the service padres did *not* have a good press. So privilege was to be abolished and religion left out. Few people today can remember the time when the working-class people of Britain were afraid to be ill because they could not afford the hospital bills. The soldiers were determined to see that that kind of life did not re-emerge.

So, at the end of the war, Churchill went out and the Labour Government came in. The reforms were introduced: the 1942 Beveridge Report was implemented. A new society *was* created, and it was a better society, a more just society. Payments were introduced for mothers bringing life into the world, and at the other end of life there was a pension for the widow. There were unemployment allowances and retirement pensions. Old people's homes proliferated and the conditions in them steadily improved as a fresh understanding of their particular needs was gained. It was a new society in which most of man's physical needs were supplied by the State. God was left out. There was nothing left for him to do. Church attendance plummeted and Sunday Schools dwindled.

Now the generation that engineered the whole process centred on those born in and around 1920. They grew up when Sunday School was still influential. Even after the

THE UK CHURCH TODAY

1920			
	SUNDAY SCHOOLS	Today's 60-year-olds. Born about 1920. Fought in World War 2. Brought in the Welfare State. Enough Sunday School and church influence to keep them in the church.	
1930			
1940	**WORLD WAR 2**	Today's 50-year-olds. Just a taste of Sunday School, not enough to keep them in the church. Now facing death and marital problems. Can't cope. Not in the church.	
	THE GENERAL ELECTION: The Welfare State is born.		
1950	**COMPLACENCY**	Today's 40-year-olds. Disturbed childhood in war years. Divorce rate 1979 34.2%. Not in the church.	
	1957 Sir Charles Darwin writes 'The present golden age'.	Today's 30-year-olds. No religious background. Observation shows them that life without God doesn't work. Returning to church.	
1960	**GROWING DOUBTS**		Today's 20-year-olds. In church, asking questions.
1970			
	DEATH/DIVORCE	**DISILLUSIONMENT**	
1980	55+ year-olds holding on in the churches.	30—55-year-olds missing from church.	15—30-year-olds moving into the churches.

events of the war they still had a bit of religion left to them. Not much, but often it was enough to keep a good many of them still going to church. But those born in the following decade were not so fortunate. They were ten years old or so when war broke out and already the Sunday Schools were in decline. Church life in general was disorganized, home life chaotic and, of course, their parents' religion almost non-existent. They grew up without God. But then they didn't need God. The new society, brought into existence by their parents, met all their requirements. Or so it seemed.

As the years passed, the situation gradually changed. At first, all appeared to be going according to plan. Britain struggled into the early fifties and out of the threat of total economic disaster. In real terms most people, and certainly all the working-class people, were better off. In 1957 a remarkable article was published in *The New Scientist* by Sir Charles Darwin, grandson of the Darwin of evolution fame. The article was called 'This present golden age'. That is an indication of how life seemed in Britain in 1957.

But it would not be unreasonable to mark 1957 as the watershed. No-one, absolutely no-one in his senses, could write such an article, with such a title, today. The golden age has vanished.

In the 1960s the economy began to falter. The Empire disintegrated. The good life wasn't quite as all-satisfying as had been expected. Those who had lived through the war lurched into their fifties and sixties and began to die. While the State attended to the cost of the funeral it had nothing to say to the dying man. It could not explain death to him. Life – but life with an inevitable and apparently meaningless death at the end of it – became an enigma, a puzzle. The war generation could not cope with death.

The generation that had followed them, the post-war generation, got married, but when couples reached the dangerous forties it soon became apparent that they couldn't cope with marriage. There were no religious sanctions to make them stay with their partners and so marriage began to fall apart. The State obligingly made divorce much easier to obtain. It was all right for the men: they found new and willing partners, and went on from there. The women were not so fortunate, nor the children. Divorce rates went up. By 1980 they had already reached 34%, and that figure was quite apart from all those marriages that simply ended in separation. The broken home became endemic. The post-war generation couldn't cope with the most fundamental of human relationships: marriage.

Meanwhile another generation was coming along. Born in the sixties, they had the opportunity of observing at first hand the consequences of living life without God. They found that their grandparents couldn't cope with death and their parents couldn't cope with marriage. A survey of young people in England, taken during the seventies, showed that these were the two great issues which concerned them: death and marriage.

So the young people began to drift back to the churches. They didn't *join* the churches, but they sat quietly, listening and waiting to see if the church had anything to offer, any answer to give to the enigmas of life, or if the church was, as they had always been told, irrelevant. In some churches their stay was brief. The language they heard was archaic, the music insipid, the sermons irrelevant. In others, *and often in churches which were aware of Church Growth concepts,* the young people stayed. They were encouraged to question, to probe, to think. New forms of worship began to emerge alongside the older forms. The older people gave a bit, encouraging the young people in their own style of worship. The young people gave a bit, turning up to the traditional services and honestly seeking to understand them, and to enjoy them.

This is one responsive group in Britain today, and the church ought to concentrate its resources on this group.

What has proved to be particularly exciting about this development is the realization that where the needs of the young people are being met, the young people then attract their parents to church: parents who have often long since

60

realized the inadequacy of their own resources for life and who will turn back to the church if only they can be sure that the church will honestly try to answer *their* questions, understand *them* and speak *their* language.

Soil testing

So there seems to be at least one group of people which can be seen to be responsive, and the observation covers many parts of Britain. But it is for each local church to identify particular groups in its own community which are responsive to the Good News. Youth clubs need to be confronted with Christ. The Good News must be taken into old people's homes. There are the bewildered immigrants, often faced with the hostility of neighbours, who need to be assured that the church, at least, offers love, sympathy, friendship and help.

It is not always easy to identify these locally responsive groups. Church Growth thinking sometimes makes use of the illustration of 'soil testing' to indicate how such groups might be recognized. The illustration comes from farming. If we have soil of a certain kind and weather of a certain kind in *this* area, and *this* particular seed does well, it is reasonable to suppose that the same seed will do well in another part of the country where the same type of soil and the same climate occur.

Similarly, if the Good News spoken in a youth club in Southend proves effective and a similar kind of youth club exists in Northend, catering for much the same sort of young people, then it is reasonable to suppose that the Good News will be fruitful there, too (SS). It is reasonable. If the Good News is not proving effective it might be a good idea to investigate the farming methodology: the way in which the seed is being planted, or watered, or weeded.

What we do need is the expectancy that looks to God for the moving of his Spirit, and an obedience that sees what God is doing and then commits the church's resources, whole-heartedly, to the task.

Of course there is a danger lurking behind this fourth

principle of Church Growth thinking. The 'responding' groups are sometimes groups favoured by the churches because they are 'our kind of people'. Other groups never even get the chance to respond because they never hear. They are considered too tough, too different – maybe even a potential threat to the smooth running of the church. But *all* must hear. The church is sent to *all* the world. There must be no surrender of this 'all' in favour of a cosy concentration on amenable people 'just like us'.

NOW WHAT DO WE DO?

1. Let's start with the young people. They do so often appear to be the ones who are looking for answers to some very important questions. But what *are* their questions, and are we tackling them?

Take this list of questions and use it as a question-naire firstly for the young people who come to church and then for a YP survey in the area. Simply ask them to pick out which is the *most* important question on your list and which is the *least* important question on the list. If you can put together a more relevant list, then do so and use that.

    i. Why is the church so divided into
       denominations? _____
   ii. How can we avoid a third world war?
       Can ordinary people do anything? _____
  iii. How can I get to know God? _____
   iv. How can I be sure that the Bible is
       right? _____
    v. I have to make so many choices in my
       life. How can I be sure that I make the
       right decisions? _____
   vi. Why is the world in such a mess? _____
  vii. How should I choose my partner
       when I get married? _____
 viii. What's wrong with drugs, smoking,
       drink? _____
   ix. What happens when I die? _____
    x. Are all religions really the same? _____

Now look at the results of your survey.

a. Compare the results obtained from your own YP with those obtained from general YP in the area. Are there any significant differences? If there are any, try to find out how those differences have appeared.

b. Is the church dealing with the vital questions in its YP programme?

c. What are the right answers to these questions? Set up a discussion group (divide if you get larger than about 10) to work through the questions. Make sure that all those involved with the YP are also involved with your discussions.

2. Find out what is happening in the local churches. Are they having a response from some particular group of people? Locate all the old people's homes, youth clubs, political clubs, and community associations (rate-payers associations?) in the area. Do you have any contact with them? Are there any plans to share Christian insights which might bear on their problems?

3. In his book *Built as a city* (see pages 36–47), David Sheppard comments on the fact that churches as a whole are not much good at reaching anyone except the 'middle classes' (whatever they are). Is this true in your area?

How would you describe the sort of people who come to your church? Are they a reasonable cross-section of the community? If not, why not?

a. We have no planned outreach to the district.

b. Others ('working class', 'upper crust') would feel uncomfortable in our church.

c. 'Like attracts like' and that is why we're a one-class church.

d. It is inevitable: Christianity always hikes people up a class or else knocks them down a class.

Discuss your answers. What changes in the church would be needed to bring in people who don't come at present? Would those changes affect people who *do* come now? So?

5
Crossing cultural barriers

I sat one Sunday morning in my car, outside the church where I was to preach. I had arrived rather too early and I was enjoying the opportunity of quiet before going in. Already a few people had arrived. But my attention was caught by the rather odd behaviour of a man who was walking towards me. But he wasn't looking at me: his whole attention was directed at the church. As he drew level with the church his head was swivelled right round, and he slowed down, obviously wanting to get a good look inside. Then he quickened his pace and walked on up the road. A short way up the road he turned and walked back towards me. Again, as he reached the church he slowed down, twisting his neck to get a good look inside, and then went on past the church in the direction from which he had first come. Yet again he turned and walked past the church. By now I had realized what was going on. He wanted to go to church, but he simply didn't know what went on inside those church doors. Like a good many men (women are very much more enterprising), he was uneasy about the unfamiliar.

In the old days, when the church hatched, matched and despatched in very large numbers, almost everybody knew what a church was like on the inside. But that is no longer the case. Many people just do not know what goes on in there. Do you have to pay at the door? Is there a place to put your coat? Can you sit anywhere? Is there someone who will show you what to do?

The church building is a good example of a cultural barrier which comes between the individual who is not a Christian and the possibility of his hearing the Good News. *In coming to Christ, people ought not to be expected to cross unnecessary cultural barriers*. This is not quite the way in which this principle is expressed by, for example, Dr McGavran. He states that people 'prefer to make their commitment to Christ without crossing cultural barriers'. That is true, but of course in coming to Christ they will always have to cross *some* cultural barriers. There are many Christian life-styles and there are many non-Christian or un-Christian life-styles, but no Christian life-style exactly matches any of the non-Christian life-styles. Becoming a Christian is certainly going to mean change: abandoning some of the things which I now do and doing some things which at present I do not do.

The fact is that Christianity challenges *all* cultures. It expresses its challenge in differing areas, depending on the culture, but all cultures are challenged at some point, on some assumption, some practice. One may be challenged on its materialism, another on its concept of marriage, another on its work-ethic. Becoming a Christian does mean cultural change.

But Church Growth thinking points out the rather obvious fact that people who wish to come to Christ should not be expected to cross *unnecessary* cultural barriers. The church building may itself be one such unnecessary cultural barrier. And this observation may well lead us on to question a common assumption, that people who want to become Christians ought to go to church. But if the church building itself puts people off and constitutes a barrier, then we may have to discover some other way of introducing people to Christ.

Three steps to church

The house group may well provide a solution to the problem. As we shall see in the next chapter, many churches are using house groups to break down large faceless congregations into smaller groups where people can really get to know one another, where they can receive appropriate teaching and where they can ask their questions without fear of being shown up in public. These house meetings can be used in a carefully thought-out programme of discipling.

Mr Christian lives in a house in Oak Avenue. Living next door, in a house that is almost a carbon copy of his, is Mr Seeker. Like everyone else, Mr Seeker has his problems but doesn't quite know where to take them. But he does know Mr Christian. He knows he is a church-goer, knows he has got a nice wife and two children, knows he enjoys football: he has seen him at the big fixtures of their local team. At step one, Mr Seeker is allowed to cross a little of the cultural barrier which necessarily separates him from the church. He goes to tea with Mr Christian.

This is quite an experience. He discovers that Mr Christian doesn't shout at his wife. Something called 'grace' is said before meals (although it is to be hoped that Mr Christian doesn't use that word and Mr Seeker simply learns that Mr Christian thanks God for his food!). Certain magazines are notably absent. Mr Seeker begins to think that there might be something in this being-a-Christian thing. The friendship develops and he starts to ask a few questions.

Step two: Mr Christian invites him to the house group. At this point care is needed. The usual house group is meant for Christians, and Mr Seeker would be entirely lost if he went to it. But every so often, say half a dozen times a year, the house group is scheduled for people like Mr Seeker. On that night some of the Christians stay away, to ensure that the Seekers do not feel threatened by the crowd of Christians who know all the answers. The programme is different, too; there's no long Bible study and no lengthy prayer session.

Step one was taken by Mr Seeker on his own, or, better, with his wife, if he had one, and maybe the children too. But step one offered no real difficulty because Mr Christian's house was just like his and the furniture probably came from the same store. Step two is not taken alone, because Mr and Mrs Christian go with him. Again the house they go into is reasonably familiar, because it is in the same area as his own. The furniture is familiar. There are more people around and he doesn't know who they are, but that is not too much of a problem because Mr Christian is there with him.

What is more, he was saved any embarrassment at the beginning because as soon as he got into the house they gave him a cup of coffee, or tea, whatever was appropriate in that particular group. He had something to do, instead of just standing around feeling conspicuous. He was secretly relieved to find that there were no hymns to be sung. There were, much to his relief, ashtrays. He relaxed in an armchair, listened to a ten-minute talk about Christianity, even chipped in an observation or two of his own as the ice began to thaw. He decided that this wasn't bad at all: he'd like to come back some time to one of the regular house group meetings.

So he went along to one of the regular meetings and liked that, too. He met a few more people and liked their conversation. What they said seemed to make sense. Now comes the acid test: he'd like to go to church.

True enough, he has already been helped to cross a number of cultural barriers which once separated him from Christianity, but even so the cultural barrier which separates him from the church is a very high one. Two things must be said about this third step into the church: first of all, the step is not as difficult as it appears, because it will be taken with Mr Christian and the friends he has made at the house group. Secondly, it is up to everyone to ensure that there really is a correspondence between all that has been said about Christianity at the house group and the things he is going to hear and see at the church. If the church is all tradition and apparently irrelevant, then step three can be disastrous: 'I thought so. This is just what I always thought religion was like. The rest of it, the house groups business, that was just window-dressing to get me here.'

And Mr Seeker never comes back.

THREE STEPS TO CHURCH

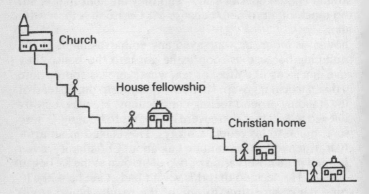

Three steps to church... but the results depend on the honesty and authenticity of every Christian along the way.

Just a word about forming house groups. If the people in the groups are really going to get to know one another, they should meet one another in the normal course of shopping or catching the train or whatever during the week. So house groups are best arranged on a geographical basis. Of course just *how* the division is made will depend on how wide-flung the congregation is. Normally you would want about thirty people living in each of the areas, because you won't find that they will all come at the beginning. And if too many do start turning up, then you need to divide up again.

But you cannot *make* people go to the house group you appoint them to. If they don't like it then they won't go. Rather quickly each house group develops its own character-istics, and people tend to shift around until they find the group they enjoy most. Encourage people to do so! If you don't and try to insist on them going to the group in *their* area when they don't like it, they will retaliate by going nowhere.

I don't think that house groups should be all of one sort together, all men, or all young people, or all teachers. In the mixed house group everyone learns from everyone else and the Christians from one area are pulled together in a way that the church meetings cannot really match. Unless, of course, the church meeting is so small as to be really a house fellowship that just happens to be held in the church building!

Of course church buildings are not the only cultural barriers which non-Christians may have to cross. There is the problem of church language. So many professional Christians find it difficult to talk about their faith without relapsing into an unnatural tone of voice, an unnatural intonation pattern and an unnatural vocabulary. Church Secretaries rarely report that someone is ill: 'Our brother Mr Thomson is laid on one side' (will someone please turn him over!). Children are not to be taught about God, but 'brought up in the nurture and admonition of the Lord'. The preacher does not arrive safely, he is 'granted travelling mercies'. Prayers are still liberally sprinkled with 'Thee's and 'Thou's. The language of the Authorized Version *is* majestic, but even the Archbishop of Canterbury recently admitted that when he wants to *understand* the Bible he reads the New English Bible.

> 'I drive a bus, ycs that's my job at sixty quid a week,
> I'm a sinner, so they tell me, one what Jesus came
>   to seek;
> So the Parson says and 'e's the bloke what really ought
>   to know
> With 'is everlasting sermons. 'e's the bloke what runs
>   the show
> At the church down in the 'igh Street, Zion Chapel,
>   that's the name,

Methodist, or maybe Baptist, I don't know, they're all
the same:
"Services at ten and six, and wear a suit, men, if you
please;
If you've got a cold don't come, or if you do don't dare
to sneeze"
'cos the Vicar doesn't like it, and 'e makes an
awful fuss,
But you 'ave to treat folks different when you're driver
of a bus.
I've often thought I'd like to be a Christian, just
like you,
With a hymn book in me 'and, and maybe learn a
prayer or two;
Course I'd 'ave to learn the language, all them "thees"
and "thous" and "thuses"
And the "shalts" and "shouldsts" and "mayests",
we don't use 'em on the buses.
Yes, I'd like to be a Christian, if the Christians spoke
like us,
But you 'ave to talk like humans when you're driver
of the bus.'

Unnecessary cultural barriers may also include dress.
Back in the 1940s, when I became a Christian, the first thing
that a new convert was expected to do was to buy a sober
suit and to provide himself with *black* shoes for Sunday.
Styles have changed and suits may be on the way out, but it
is surprising how many people in the churches still feel that
it is somehow a religious thing to wear a suit on Sunday, and
faintly irreverent to turn up in a polo-necked sweater, or
jeans. I still relish the comment of one shocked Christian
when young people started to move into the church of
which I was pastor in Addis Ababa. They came in all their
marvellous variety, tight jeans, bushy hair, sandals. She
looked at them all in a kind of shock disbelief and then said
to her companion, 'Look at that; they're letting *anyone* into
the church now'!

Even singing may prove to be a cultural barrier. It used to be common for even non-church-goers to gather around the piano on a Saturday night and sing songs, even hymns. It used to be the practice to sing 'Abide with me' at the Wembley Cup Final. But a new life-style has swept those things away. The television has disposed of the Saturday night sing and 'choruses' have made their appearance on the football terraces. I wonder how those choruses are created? I wonder who starts them? I wonder why so many of them are obviously created out of evangelical choruses? I wonder how the words are learnt?

If singing is something of an anachronism today it is surely worth questioning the use of hymns at evangelistic meetings. Unless, of course, at evangelistic meetings we are really only dealing with the lapsed, with the fringe element of the Christian church who can cope with hymn singing. But it could well be that it is precisely the hymn singing that puts us off inviting the *real* heathen to evangelistic meetings. It would seem to me that there is a place here for the straightforward *lecture* or talk, without all the trimmings. Simply an attempt to make quite clear to those who come what Christianity has to say about, say, death and dying, or the Trade Unions, or marriage, or unemployment, or how to bring up children, or the Ten Commandments, or whatever.

There is, in fact, quite a movement towards such meetings, arranged by a local group of churches, crossing denominational barriers, located on neutral territory in, say, a school. This kind of joint planning makes much better use of the comparatively small number of Christians who are equipped to speak at such meetings. It can be frustrating to be invited to speak on a subject of real importance, and then subsequently to be invited to repeat the talk for three or four other churches in the same area. It is poor stewardship, and can be discouraging for all who attend if each gathering has only twenty people, where better co-operation would have produced one meeting with a couple of hundred people.

Unnecessary cultural barriers. Ministers and congregations need to look carefully at what they expect of the unchurched when they lay their plans for evangelism. The *first* consideration ought to be the people we are expecting to come. Usually they are the last to be considered.

NOW WHAT DO WE DO?

1. Ten Commandments for successful house groups
Since this chapter has been largely about the use of house groups, let us look at a few of the steps to be taken if you're intending to start them.

1. Establish goals. Decide what the groups are for. You do not need to keep the same goal for ever. In fact the first goal may well be 'to establish a family feeling', or 'fellowship'. But that won't do in the long term. People won't keep coming just for a cup of coffee and a bit of a chat. So a mid-term goal is needed. Prayer? Bible study? Sharing? Evangelism? Avoid having two or three goals for one meeting.

2. Make sure that you know how the goals are to be scored. Who is going to *teach*? How is she supposed to *learn*?

3. Arrange a monitoring process. In other words, you must have some way of finding out how things are going in the groups. *Not* through the report of the house group leader, by the way. Either have someone independent going the rounds, or better still, design a simple fill-in-the-blanks card which can be handed out one evening for everyone to fill in — anonymously, perhaps.

4. Success is potentially disastrous! The group grows and gets too big and then everyone stops asking questions and you don't know one another and you're back to square one. Split! Of course this will be resisted and it does mean finding a new leader as good as the present one. But do it if you can.

5. Break the ice by getting people involved. Do the washing up together; don't leave it until everyone has gone home, except the poor couple who live

there. If the back fence has blown down, then put it up together.

6. Get people to prepare for any kind of study *before* they come, even if it is just to read a chapter from the Bible. Distribute a sheet of comments with a few blanks to be filled in.

7. If questions are to be used, they need very careful preparation by the leader. If the answer is obvious, then no adult will try to give it: 'Surely there must be a catch somewhere.' 'What do you think about…?' is a good way to start a question. 'Who…?' is not.

8. Prayer. Don't expect people to remember all the people and problems you mention. Write them on a large sheet of paper (say 2ft by 3ft) and then encourage people to look up *during the prayer session* to refresh their memories. And be specific. 'Let's pray for our missionaries' is hopeless. 'John is ill at present. Let's pray that they'll be able to get him up to Nairobi to the hospital quickly' is meaningful.

9. Stop before people are fidgety. It is far better to stop too soon ('Oh, we could have gone on for another hour') than too late ('Cor, thought he would never stop!').

10. Break up the evening into bite-sized chunks, according to the bite of your members. For some groups the chunks cannot be more than 10 minutes (coffee, reading, talk, discussion, sharing of prayer requests, prayer, planning for next time…that is over an hour's programme already), but others will want fewer interruptions.

2. Relevant worship

What *is* worship? Obviously it ought to have some-thing to do with what goes on in church on Sunday. But what *is* it? Is it what you do? Or what you feel? Or a bit of both? Read Exodus 33:7–10; John 4:19–24 and Revelation 7:9–12. Try also a dictionary definition.

What would you mean by a *good* Sunday service? How would you recognize a church service that was 'irrelevant'? What do you mean by a 'relevant' church service?

3. From the other side

Write down *five* things about your Sunday services that your nearest non-Christian neighbour would find odd. Is it possible to change any of these so as to lower the barriers for him? If not, why not? Clerical collars? Archaic language? The collection? Sitting in rows? Hard seats? Hats? Hymns?

4. Working with other Christians

a. Write down as complete a list as possible of all Christian activities in the area: names of churches, school Christian Unions, Mission society offices, Salvation Army, and so on.

b. Now write down any activities you share in with them.

c. Are you satisfied? Could you put a bit more into it?

d. Are there other things you could do together? A joint sing-in on a Saturday night? A united choir for Easter or Christmas? Surely you can do *something* to show that we really are all one in Christ Jesus?

e. Is there a pressing social need, locally, that we could all be involved in?

5. Something to read

Eddie Gibbs' Grove Booklet no. 64. *Grow through groups,* is the thing to read. Note especially what he says on pages 10–11 on the dangers of home groups: introversion, fragmentation and stagnation. Examine your church for groups which exhibit these tendencies. Why have they developed? What can be done to put things right?

6.

Spoiling the Egyptians

General Booth said that he could not see why the Devil should have all the best tunes, so the Salvation Army took the tunes and put Christian words to them. This is what I mean by spoiling the Egyptians: making use of whatever is to hand, provided always that it can be shown to conform to our two basics: the sovereignty of the Holy Spirit and the authority of the Bible.

The Church Growth movement suggests that if we are to develop responsible and effective patterns of Christian witness we need to keep up to date with the new insights into what makes society tick. I imagine that everyone would accept the suggestion that our methods of evangelism could be improved, but often we are simply not taking notice of powerful new discoveries about society which in no way contradict our Christian principles.

Now the Christian is not entirely free from those principles which are found to govern the rest of society. He is not free from basic financial principles: Income five pounds, expenditure four pounds ninety-nine pence: bliss. Income five pounds, expenditure five pounds and one penny: eventual ruin. That applies to the Christian as well as to the unchurched, it applies to the missionary society as well as to a multi-national corporation, it applies to the local church as well as to the national churches.

We need to be aware of the role of inflation. Churches often live in a fool's paradise, thinking that their income is increasing because the number of pounds being given is increasing. But in 1979 it would have been necessary for income to increase by something like 20% even to keep pace with inflation. And it is by no means uncommon to find church members downright annoyed if a proudly displayed rising graph is turned into a dismally plunging one by applying a correction for inflation. They seem to feel that inflation-correction is unspiritual.

Of course care is needed with statistics. Facts are facts, but this science of statistics is really concerned with the presentation and interpretation of facts about numbers. Interpretation, in Church Growth terms, is usually a spiritual exercise, requiring spiritual discernment.

For example, Church Growth books often suggest the preparation of *population profiles*. This exercise is simply a way of showing how many men and how many women there are in each age group of the population. A profile is prepared for the district and another is prepared for the church and the two are then compared. At the point of comparison it is often assumed, without any justification at all, that the two profiles should be similar. But, to take a parallel situation, if a population profile from a local factory was taken and compared with the community profile there would be precious few similarities. The dissimilarity is to be expected because the two environments are different. The history of the factory is not the same as that of the community. The purpose of the factory is not the same as that of the community as a whole.

If we consider the church, we can see already, from what was said in chapter four, that the profile would probably show few people from the 'middlies', people in their late forties and fifties. It would be quite illegitimate to look at the profile and say that the church was not doing enough to reach the forties and fifties, without taking into account

76

COMMUNITY AND CONGREGATION PROFILES

These figures are for a particular community and a 'model' congregation, and conform generally to the UK pattern of distribution.

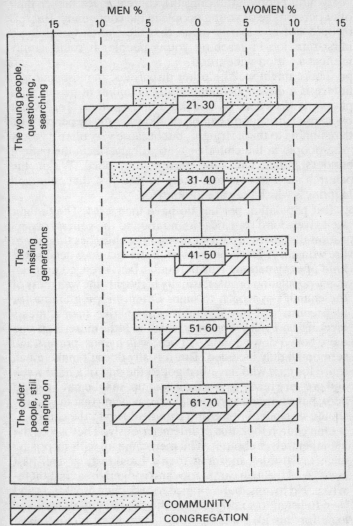

other factors which might explain their absence. On the other hand we might find an unexpectedly high percentage of young people attending the church, much higher than the percentage of young people in the community. But this would not necessarily mean that the church was doing a first-rate job in reaching young people. It could simply reflect a nation-wide trend.

There might well be other disparities. In most churches there is a disproportionately high number of people with nervous disorders of one kind and another. This is not because Christianity can be swallowed only by people who are unable to think straight, but because very often it is only the people in the churches who will give them the patient understanding and support that they need. Within the church such people are likely to find just that calm and kindness which they are looking for.

But population profiles do have their uses. They might well give a hard statistical foundation to the general observation that there are fewer men in the churches than there are women. A *fact* is only a fact, but a fact does need some kind of explanation. This particular fact, dredged up from many population profiles, usually highlights the weakness of the church's approach to men. Often the programme for men consists of nothing more imaginative than a men's meeting on Friday evening, which is little more than one more boiled-down Sunday service, with hymns, prayers and sermon all duly included. But it really doesn't make much sense for men who have just got to the end of a hard week and are very ready to put their feet up, maybe have a good yarn, but who need a great deal of convincing that they really should turn out of home and trundle down to the church.

One church took this problem seriously. They asked the men themselves about it. The men came up with surprising idea: a Saturday morning men's breakfast, at half-past eight. And the men came, too, and cooked breakfast themselves. No hymns, but a chance to talk over breakfast, and then to listen to someone over the second cup of tea. The logic for this idea was obvious. They lived in south-east

78

London, on the very edge of the commuter belt. They had something like an hour and a half between leaving work and reaching home. So they arrived home at about 7.15. Then it was time for a meal. And after that, who really wanted to go out again? Especially in winter.

But Saturday morning? Well, you're just under everyone's feet in the morning. There's time to get out into the garden in the afternoon, and the meeting at the church finished early enough for everyone to get home in plenty of time for dinner.

So, the fifth principle of Church Growth thinking is that *the insights of sociology, statistics, group dynamics, may all be used in developing Christian mission.*

How the church can use groups

Man is gregarious. He functions best, most happily, in groups. It is a biblical principle that it is not good for people to be alone. Incidentally, that is why solitary confinement is an un-Christian concept of punishment: it denies to the victim a vital element of his human-ness.

Man functions well in groups. First it is in the family. Then he learns to work in classes at school. He forms tennis clubs, soccer clubs. He develops some kind of team approach to his work.

Having said that, it is important to recognize that a person's behaviour is to some extent determined by the group that he is with. The study of group behaviour is called group dynamics. For it is a simple fact that we behave differently when we are alone, differently when we are with a small group of a dozen or so, differently again when we are with a larger group of, say, fifty.

In fact we may identify four basic group sizes:

G1, the family-size group or *familiar* group;
G2, the *small* group;
G3, the *large* group;
G4, the *crowd*.

The sizes of these groups can be defined rather precisely: G1 from 2 to 6, G2 from 7 to 16, G3 from 25 to 80 and G4 when there are more than 100 people. A little careful observation will soon convince anyone of the reality of these different groupings, and of the different effects produced on the individual by the group sizes.

GROUP DYNAMICS

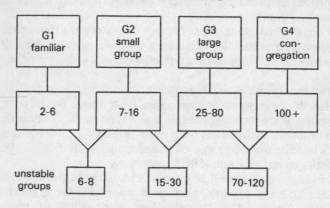

If groups in the 'unstable' category meet regularly the group size will tend to shift to a more stable number. Which way group size will change will be decided by the dynamics of the situation. A *growing* group will quickly jump the gap. A declining group will slide further down. In either case it is vital that the group leader be aware of the new dynamics of the group.

It is interesting to notice the existence of four groups, roughly corresponding to our four groups, amongst the followers of Jesus. The G2 group is obvious, the twelve; but from amongst the twelve there was an inner G1 group consisting of Peter, James and John, sometimes with Andrew added in. Then Luke 10:1–17 refers to a G3 group of 70 (or maybe 72). And then, of course, there was the 'great crowd of his disciples', a G4 grouping, mentioned repeatedly (but see, for example, Luke 6:17 where the 'great crowd' of his disciples is differentiated from the multitude of the merely curious).

The four groups

The *familiar group*, the group that is of family size, demonstrates the importance of individuality. In the family each person is a distinct individual. With the exception of identical twins it is very rare to find two children in a family who behave similarly. Families have the authority-figure, usually the father, but sometimes the mother; the protective-figure, usually the mother, but sometimes the father; the good-boy, who may be a girl, and the bad-boy, the clever one and the disobedient one, the lazy one and the industrious one, and so on. The number of available roles is enormous and the family presents a range of these roles, a range which is partly determined by inheritance, partly determined by the roles of other members of the family, and partly determined by the environment.

The G2 group, the *small group*, is the next stage along in group size, and already demonstrates the way in which individual personality begins to be submerged under the pressure of the group. Such a group will allow a group leader to emerge, corresponding to the authority-figure of the G1 group. The individual members, however, tend to fall into only two sub-sets, those who back the group leader and those who do not. But the individualism of the G1 group is much less prominent. The G2 group is important, because in this group it is possible to have one person to be an authoritative speaker, but for the rest of the group to feel free to disagree with him or to ask questions when he is not understood. The authority of the leader is recognized, but the group members are not intimidated by it.

The G3 or *large group* sees a further devaluation of the individual. Once again there will be a group leader, but he will now have a small group of more-or-less official backers, and the rest of the group will tend to become anonymous members. In the G2 size it was possible for every member of the group to know well every other member of the group personally. In the G3 group it is just possible to know every member of the group by sight, to know the majority by name, but G2 groups within the larger group will inevitably form to provide the social links which are a necessary part of life. In addressing the G3 size of group a more formal type of speech is already necessary if everyone is to hear clearly. Conversation goes out. Few people will ask questions in the G3 situation, precisely because a more formal type of speech is required. The handful of people in the group who know how to speak in a G3 situation might ask a question if invited to do so, but most of the rest, however much they may be encouraged to speak up, will remain quiet. The G3 situation is somewhat threatening to its members.

At the G4 level we reach *crowd size,* and the psychology of crowds is a fascinating study. A crowd may often behave almost as one, even though no leader is apparent. The crowd may assume the behaviour-patterns of an individual, responding as one even though the individuals who make up the crowd might individually have responded differently. The G4 experience is often an exciting experience. One is carried away, drawn out of oneself. The inhibitions of the individual are lost in the essential anonymity of the crowd. In the G4 situation oratory is called for, or at least oratory becomes possible. Oratory in a G2 situation is simply absurd.

The church and the four groups

Each of the four group sizes provides a necessary kind of structure or learning experience for those involved. Churches ought to provide the G1, the G2, the G3 and the G4 experience for all their members. At the lowest end of the scale, churches ought to ensure that young Christians, students away from home or Christians who come from homes that are not Christian, unmarrieds, old folks who are widows or widowers, should somewhere have a family to relate to. It is not enough to assure such people that the church is very friendly and they would always be welcome to drop in for a cup of tea. What is needed is *a* particular family. The intention is *not* that they should be removed from their own home situations, but that they should have a family to relate to somewhere. True incorporation into a family would mean having a key to the front door and really being free to drop in and not merely *have* a cup of tea, but being sufficiently free to *make* a cup of tea!

At the other end of the scale, each church should ensure that its members enjoy the G4 experience: 'Celebration', as some writers call it. Christians who worship in small churches with small congregations begin to think small, to get the idea that churches are all small, and this can lead to the conviction that the church is a dying business. So the small churches should ensure that somehow the G4 situation is provided. Some churches arrange this by closing down their evening service one Sunday in each month, and the whole congregation goes off together to worship with a bigger congregation. Elsewhere several small congregations join up once a month, or once a quarter, on a Saturday, for a rally of some kind. The emphasis does not have to be on some great speaker; rather it is on inspiration, with plenty of good singing, maybe a joint choir, and everyone who plays an instrument brings it along to help with the sense of community.

It should be obvious that the larger churches have a responsibility here, to share their existing celebration events with other Christians, but not necessarily to foist their ministers on the smaller churches. A certain measure of humility is called for in this sharing.

The G3, or large group, is a very common size of group in churches. In fact, according to David Wasdell of Urban Church Project, it is the most commonly occurring size of congregation in the Anglican churches. The advantage of the G3 group is that it is large enough to be able to sing without individuals sounding too conspicuous, large enough to be able (just) to support a minister and a building, but small enough to enable everyone to know everybody else's name. The disadvantage is that the group is too large to allow for the congregation to take much of an active part in

83

worship. The group size inhibits questions from the congregation.

So what is needed for the G3 congregation is some kind of G2 experience. The larger group needs to be divided up. One way of doing this is to introduce house groups.

But the significance of the four group sizes does not lie so much in this identification of the actual value of each group size, but in identifying the problems which arise when the required group behaviour does not match up with group dynamics.

For example, I recently preached in a church in London. The church seats about 500, and at the turn of the century it used to be full. The minister preached from a rather high pulpit, because one third of his congregation would be in an upstairs gallery. So his pulpit was about on a level with the gallery: he could see everyone and he could be seen by everyone. But when I went to the church, the congregation totalled about thirty. There were only three in the upstairs gallery. Just as in the good old days, I was solemnly led into the church, the door to the pulpit was opened, I ascended the hill of the Lord and the door was shut behind me. When I stood up to begin the service, having thus far been aware of a congregation of only three, I discovered the other twenty-seven, scattered in the four corners of the church. And I was expected to preach to them – from the pulpit.

After the service I asked the Church Secretary if he would object to my leading the evening service from downstairs. He was most put out, almost shocked. 'We *always* lead the service from the pulpit'! And I had to do so, again.

Now such a church must die. It is expecting its members to behave unnaturally. When you join a group of six or seven people (and in this church we actually had four such sub-groups, clustered in different parts of the church), you greet them – but not if the group meets in church. And when one addresses a small group one does so in a more-or-less natural tone. It is not necessary to shout to make yourself heard by thirty people – unless you happen to be in church. In this unnatural situation it is only the especially

84

committed who remain: the wife of the minister (if they have one), the wives of the elders or deacons, people who have attended the church for many years, people who are too old to make the change to another church. But a newcomer will attend once only.

What is needed in such a situation is for the church to recognize the absurdity of carrying on in a G2 or even a G3 situation as though it were a G4 situation. Only when the conduct of the group gathering is appropriate to the group size will the group be able to respond naturally, and only then will the group feel free to introduce new members, or new members be likely to remain.

There is also the importance of the role of the actual environment: the size of the church or hall in relationship to the size of the group. To have twenty people meeting in a church built for 400 is discouraging for the twenty and intimidating for anyone who is tentatively considering joining the church. Group dynamics would indicate that a dwindling congregation in an over-sized building will have the decline accelerated by the inappropriate building.

A large Anglican church in Blackpool and another in West London had just this problem. In each case the dynamics of the local population had changed. Whereas the churches had originally existed in the middle of areas of dense population, they now found themselves stranded, de-populated. Congregation sizes fell. Both churches, independently, took similar action. One end of the church was blocked off. The central part, which had been part of the nave, became a lounge, seating about a hundred. There was wall-to-wall carpeting and comfortable chairs. In the London church one aisle became a well-equipped kitchen, with a sliding hatch through to the new lounge. The other aisle was turned into blackboard-equipped classrooms for the church's education programme. When the congregation at the evening service dropped to about sixty, they moved into the lounge. The new environment dramatically changed things. Sixty filled the lounge comfortably. The decline in numbers was arrested. Numbers began to increase. And when I visited the church they were already finding the lounge too small. But they were delaying the move back into the church until the lounge was really packed, when the 120 or so congregation would be a reasonable size to put into the diminished church building, and when the dynamic of a *growing* congregation should enable them to continue to grow. It is valuable here to notice the danger of delaying a move too long. A building can inhibit growth: congregations tend to grow until the accommodation is filled and then to stop. If this congregation reaches a full house...and then delays the move into the sanctuary until congregation size is stabilized, it could find the condition of stability fixed.

The appropriate use of the G2 group

It is very much easier to preach a sermon than it is to run a house group effectively. The house group is usually the most effective way of providing for the G2 experience in any church. But our general lack of understanding of the dynamics of the G2 group often leads to the abuse of the house group and to the failure of the group to realize its full potential.

Very often those who start house groups have a fear that the groups will be led into heresy. And so some authority-figure has to be appointed to run the groups; a deacon, an elder, someone from the PCC. Now a person may be an excellent church officer but a disaster as a group leader. In particular, a person may be an excellent preacher but entirely the wrong person to lead a group. The reason is rather obvious: he is accustomed to leading, actually to *dominating*, to taking something of a solo role, and is almost certainly going to lead, to dominate, to take the solo role in the small group. And that is just where dominating personalities can be a disaster.

However, it *is* important that in house groups there should be someone to lead, and someone who knows the right answers to the kind of issues that are likely to be discussed. There is a naïve belief among many of those who push house groups that *knowledge* is unimportant, even

86

undesirable: 'You bring your nothing and I'll bring my nothing and we'll have a discussion and somehow, because we're a group, nothing plus nothing will equal something.' It won't. In a group there is a need for someone who knows some right answers, so that if error appears he can correct it.

The person who knows the right answers *might* be the group leader, but not necessarily so. The group leader is essentially someone who can put people at ease, encouraging everyone to share; who can sum up ideas and clarify them for those who are not too good at formulating their ideas clearly, who can ask stimulating questions, *real* questions, not questions to which the answers are so obvious that no-one will answer, either because the question seems an insult to intelligence or because everyone feels that there must be a catch somewhere. Questions should be the kind that make people think but to which there are real answers.

As in all groups, there must be a clearly-defined purpose for the house group. This does need some careful attention, since there are several quite legitimate goals for a house group. As we have seen, the group may be used for Christians or it may be used for introducing the unchurched to Christianity. The goal may be primarily fellowship, or it may be prayer, or it may be instruction. It is not a bad idea for any group to write down in a single sentence what its primary task is, and then to review its activities every six months to see whether the activities or the task need revision.

Discussion in a small group will not begin without some kind of initial input, something to get people talking. If the group will co-operate, pre-meeting private study is helpful, especially if some kind of duplicated guide can be distributed, with an indication of the parts of the Bible that might be read, the chapter of a book that might be consulted and a few initial questions to be tackled. If this is not possible, then a brief introduction to the topic under discussion is in order at the beginning of the group meeting. The emphasis is on *brief*. The G2 group is *not* meant for sermonizing.

The G1 group: an oddity explained

One final word about the G1 group. Under normal circumstances this group size does not appear in church. But it often appears temporarily in young people's work: Crusaders, Covenanters, a Boys' Brigade Bible class, for example. Normally such classes are G2 groups. You can talk to them and they will listen, so long as you don't go on too long. They will ask questions. They will try to answer questions. But some Sundays things just do not work.

The behaviour of the children suddenly changes. They won't co-operate, won't sit still. It is not the phase of the moon nor the state of the tide, but often it is the size of the group. If the group changes from G2 to G1 the group begins to behave like a family. The young people become individuals: the bad boy emerges, the show-off begins to act up, someone else is determined to be helpful – just as if they were a family. Many Sunday School teachers have been bewildered by this phenomenon, which is quite familiar to group dynamics. The teacher who can cope with the situation is the one who can stop being the teacher (the role appropriate to a G2 situation) and can start being Mum or Dad (the role appropriate to the new G1 situation).

If we are to develop mission responsibly, then we need to 'spoil the Egyptians', to make use of the insights of statistics and group dynamics and communication theory and the rest, although always with a careful eye on Scripture to ensure that we maintain our two basic assumptions: the authority of Scripture and the sovereignty of the Spirit. We do not want merely to manipulate people. But we do need to be aware of some of the factors which *do* and *will* influence their behaviour, and to ensure that we leave the Spirit free to do what he wants to do without unnecessary barriers.

We have looked, in this chapter, primarily at two areas, the use of statistics and the use of group dynamics. We might have drawn attention also to communication theory, that helps us to understand the very complex way in which my ideas can be transmitted so as to be understood by others. Again, it is amazing in this age of visual communication that so few churches make use of visuals in their witness. The overhead projector is a remarkable tool. It has the great advantage that it can be used without blacking out the room, and it provides a very convenient way of learning new hymns without costly duplication, and with the additional advantage that everyone keeps his head up while singing. In Bible teaching the whole passage being studied can be put on an acetate and projected, and that saves a great deal of confusion when the congregation uses several different versions of the Bible.

There is also the tape-recorder. This can be used along with the church's amplifying system to bring John Stott or Billy Graham into the service. And video cassettes now make it possible for churches to study televised materials together, such as programmes on Islam, for example.

Church Growth encourages us all to make use of the new skills that are developing and to use these skills in serving God.

NOW WHAT DO WE DO?

1. Investigation
Prepare a population profile for your church and for the district. If the church has some kind of membership roll and it is representative of the people who actually come to church, you could start from that. Otherwise take a census at church on three random Sundays. It is easiest to ask *everyone* to fill in a card previously placed in the pews or on the chairs. All you need is name (this gives you the person's sex) and age (in groupings).

The population profile for the district is a little more difficult to get, but the local library should be able to advise on where the information can be obtained. Usually the Council offices have a statistical department, and they are almost always co-operative.

Remember that what you want is the *percentage*

of your total congregation that is, say, male and aged between 21 and 30. If you have a total congregation of 163 and you have 13 men aged between 21 and 30, then the percentage is $\frac{13}{163}$ x 100, which comes to 8%. Repeat the calculation for the women in the same age group, and then for all the other age groups.

It is easiest to see the results of your calculations if you use a diagram like the one on page 77. Put the figures for the church and the figures for the local population on the same diagram and then compare them.

There is no particular reason why the two sets of figures should be the same. But there should be some effort made to see if any big discrepancy between the two sets of figures is due to the church over-emphasizing one group *at the expense of another.* After all, you cannot have too many of any group in church! But an emphasis on work among young people sometimes leads to the neglect of the 'middlies'. So compare the two sets of figures, because sometimes they do point out an area of work which is being neglected. If there is such an area of neglect, what do you propose doing about it?

2. Using groups

People do seem to need what is provided by all four groups discussed in this chapter. Does everyone in the church have the chance of G1, G2, G3 and G4 sharing with other Christians? Tabulate the provision made for children, teenagers, twenties, middlies and senior citizens. Are the 'meetings' organized in a way that takes into account the group sizes? Can re-grouping along new lines make the groups more viable?

3. Using local resources

It is not necessary to have everything that is done *by* the church done *in* the church. Sometimes the building itself might be off-putting. Or maybe there are better facilities locally. Would a local school hall be better for showing Christian films? Would it even be possible to hire the cinema?

Can the church plug into existing work? Do local

play-groups need help? Or meals-on-wheels? Does the hospital need help with their library? Or their kiosk or sales trolley?

4. Using modern teaching methods

The traditional sermon really may not be the best way of teaching Christians and almost certainly is not the best way of reaching non-Christians in your church. Invite a schoolteacher to talk about modern teaching methods and then discuss how they might be used in the church. Arrange for someone to demonstrate the use of the overhead projector (OHP). Incidentally Lion Publishing, Icknield Way, Tring, Herts produce a beautiful set of OHP map transparencies for Bible teaching, and Staedtler, the firm that produces OHP supplies of all kinds, run training courses in the use of the OHP.

5. Something to read

Read Gavin Reid's book, *The gagging of God*. If your church is very certain of its message, you may already be having trouble in persuading people that changes are needed. Gavin Reid warns, on page 35 of his book: 'The trouble is that those churches that already experiment with alternatives to the sermon, often appear to be those that are unsure of their message in the first place; while those that are really firmly grounded in the gospel message are all too frequently those who are least imaginative in presenting their case.'

7
Scoring goals

The sixth principle of Church Growth thinking is that *churches should set specific goals for themselves*. One of the reasons for establishing goal-setting as a principle is that we can assess our work only where we have specific targets or known goals. Let me illustrate. At camp one year I decided to learn something about archery. There was a bow; there was a quiver filled with arrows; and there in front of me was a target. Now it is not particularly difficult to fit an arrow to the bowstring, to bend the bow and even to loose off an arrow. But an embarrassingly empty target showed me (and everyone else) that I had missed.

Of course it is very comforting to dispense with the target and simply to fire off a joyful arrow or two. No-one can then say that you missed. By the same token, you can never say that you hit. Too much church life is like archery without a target, like a walk without a destination. We don't know what we're trying to do, and at the end of the year we don't know whether we've done it or not. We can't say that we have. Comfortingly, though, no-one can say that we haven't.

As we have already seen in chapter one, if it is to continue to exist a group must have a primary task. But often the primary task of the church ('my witnesses') has been lost sight of, and the task has become simply the task of keeping afloat. The church is not getting anywhere, but at least at the year's end it is still there, with all the bills paid, with most of the members still attending and most of the meetings still being held. But surely the church ought to be not static but *dynamic*, ready to change, to move out, as fresh leading from the Spirit is given. And this is what happened to the church at Antioch. As the leaders of the church were fasting and praying, the Spirit showed them the next step for the church: to send Paul and Barnabas out as God's messengers (Acts 13:1–3). And notice what is so often overlooked: the call came to the church, not merely to Paul and Barnabas. It would seem to me reasonable to assume that the church as a whole was fasting and praying so as to determine God's next step for them.

This provides an opportunity for making a fundamental observation about goal-setting: goals must be set on your knees. They emerge out of prayer. They are not dreamed up but prayed down.

For God has plans for us:

> '*I know the plans I have for you, says the Lord, plans for welfare and not for evil, to give you a future and a hope*' (Jeremiah 29:11).

The example of Abraham shows that God is not unwilling to share his plans with us:

> '*Shall I hide from Abraham what I am about to do, seeing that Abraham shall become a great and mighty nation, and all the nations of the earth shall bless themselves by him? No, for I have chosen him...*' (Genesis 18:17–19).

So then, if God has plans and he is not unwilling to reveal his plans to us, it is not unbiblical for us to try to discern what he wants us to do and then to make our plans, which are God's plans foreshortened, so that we do his will. That was why the church at Antioch sent out two missionaries.

Goals fall into various categories. There are personal goals and community goals, there are short-term goals and long-term goals, and there are immediate goals. What do I look for in this service? What do I expect next Sunday? What do I look for by the end of this year? What should the church do now? What ought it to have done by the end of the decade?

Three characteristics of valid goals

To be of any value, goals must be *specific, acceptable* and *attainable*. Goals must be *specific* as to quality, quantity and chronology. I need to know *what* I want, *how much* I want and *when* I want to have it. The request, 'Let's pray that God will mightily bless the preaching of the Word next Sunday,' is specific as to chronology, 'next Sunday'. But what is meant by God 'blessing' the preaching? What do we expect God to *do* on Sunday? Do we expect God to bring those six new young people to faith in himself (SS)? Do we expect the two elders who have been squabbling with each other for the past fifteen years to apologize and put things right? Do we expect healing for Jill's migraines?

Of course, if the prayer is prayed regularly enough, it will eventually be possible to say that prayer was answered because eventually somebody *will* be 'blessed'. Meanwhile no-one can say that we haven't reached our goal, because the goal is sufficiently vague that we can't really recognize it. We are praying and we are planning in the fog of our own uncertainties.

Similarly, 'Let's aim at increasing our giving' is not an adequate goal. It is not specific except in terms of *quality*. I know what I want: money. But how much? and by when? And what do we really mean by that rather bland word 'increase'? Is a 5% increase really an increase if the rate of inflation is 15%? Much more to the point is something like this: 'Let's aim at increasing our giving from £120 per week to £250 per week by next Easter.' That is a measurable goal,

94

and come next Easter the congregation will know whether or not it has reached its goal.

Is such a goal merely materialistic? David Wasdell of the Anglican Church's Urban Church Project reports that, in his study of the Anglican churches, the *giving* of the church has proved to be the most sensitive indicator of its spirituality. If a church comes alive, spiritually, it will really begin to give, financially.

Of course financial goals, like all others, are set on your knees. The goal that is set is part of the revelation of God's total plan for the church. If the church is led into appointing a minister for youth, God is likely also to lead the church into financial commitment to pay him adequately. Such a church would be well advised to get on its collective knees to ask God to show them how much he expects them to contribute to the furtherance of his plans. After all, God does not normally rain down pound notes on pay day. He has his part to play and we have ours. And he is willing to show us just what our part is.

Goals must be *attainable* and *acceptable*. There is no sense in a group of Christians setting themselves unrealistic goals. Goals set by the Holy Spirit may be breath-taking in concept, but precisely because they *are* from the Spirit the church will find them acceptable. Imaginative goals which spring merely from the imagination may be impressive, but, precisely because they do spring from the imagination and not from the Spirit, the Spirit-led congregation will not be carried away by the imagination. Goals that are Spirit-led are attainable and will prove to be acceptable to the Spirit-led congregation.

Goal-setting can be an exciting experience. In recent years, churches that I have visited have accepted all kinds of goals for themselves:

To increase attendance at the mid-week Bible study to sixty within six months.

To establish a male-voice choir with at least thirty members in time for next Christmas.

To visit all the children who have been to our Sunday

95

school and Covenanter classes over the past twenty years, so far as we are able to locate them, and to arrange a reunion party on November 5th.

To begin seven house fellowships with at least twelve people regularly attending each by Easter.

To scrap the present news-sheet and produce an eight-page *Reader's Digest* sort of church magazine instead, to sell at 5p, to start at the New Year.

Other churches have been led into definite planning for planting new churches and even for specific numbers of people to be brought into the family of God through their ministry (SS). And just so long as all this planning is carried through by a church that is on its knees, it is legitimate.

There can be no doubt at all that churches which have clearly-defined goals are radically different from those which have none. A sense of vague but pious optimism is replaced by a spirit of responsibility. So often when I have been invited to preach a 'gospel message' in a church and I have asked the elders or deacons how many of the un-churched they expect to come, they reply vaguely that there will probably be some.

'But how many have *you* brought to church tonight?'

'Well, of course, we are kept very busy with our respon-sibilities as elders, but I'm sure there will be some...'

Goals can be disturbing things. They tell us what we have done and they tell us what we ought to have done and they tell us what we have left undone.

Goals are set after prayer. But who sets them? This is only a suggestion, but it seems to me that God places leaders in the church in order to *lead*. You cannot lead unless you know where you are going. Goal-setting ought to begin with the church's leadership.

But it is no use setting goals if the church members do not understand the goals or do not agree with them. The goals of the leadership need to be discussed by the church and then endorsed by the church. They must become *our* goals and not *their* goals. And in a church where there have never

96

been any goals before, it may take a bit of persuasion to get the church members to accept the new idea.

But I have seen churches come to life when once the idea of a goal is accepted. There is excitement in working with God in bringing about those purposes which he has shared with the church, awe and wonder when the goal is reached, and astonishment at being privileged to share God's work.

NOW WHAT DO WE DO?

1. Something to read
This is a rather heavy assignment, but the church ought to have at least one copy of Robin Thomson's book, already mentioned several times, *Can British churches grow?* Read Unit two, which deals almost entirely with goals and goal-setting. Set aside an evening when someone will talk about this important subject.

2. Possible goals
Over the past few years I have encountered all kinds of fascinating goals set for themselves by churches. These goals have certainly opened my eyes to the kind of things that need to be done and can be done when the Spirit moves in the churches. In addition to those already mentioned (see pages 95-96), here are some sample goals:

1. To start a twelve-piece music group (orchestra, band, or whatever) and put on a first concert at Easter.

2. To get a Christian elected to the local council. (Local Christians were concerned at the obvious humanistic bias of the local authority and its lack of concern over certain aspects of morality. It is not enough to grumble: we must be prepared to do something!)

3. To appoint a minister for youth by the end of next year.

4. To redecorate the interior of the church and replace the pews by movable chairs (the fixed pews made any kind of small group activity impossible).

C.A.—D

5. To provide an effective notice-board outside the church, with a rota of people responsible for keeping information up to date. (This church had a bus-stop right outside it and people often had a long wait...with nothing to do. The notice-board used newspaper cuttings, cartoons and photographs as well as the usual posters and announcements. Incidentally they also removed their hedge separating the church property from the pavement and put in several benches for people to sit on.)

6. To increase the church's giving so that they would be able to provide full financial support for their one missionary, instead of the current 10% of support. (Another church decided to give a scholarship to Bible college for one of their young people who was preparing for overseas mission.)

7. To increase the average attendance at the evening service from around forty to eighty in twelve months. (They did it, too. People who had previously always just 'hoped' and even prayed that others would be 'brought in', for the first time saw the need to *invite* them in and to *bring* them in.)

3. Setting goals
Discuss the seven goals listed above. Answer the following questions:

1. Why are we unwilling to set goals?

2. What is God's goal for the world (read Revelation 21–22)? What is God's goal for my life? How are these goals to be reached?

3. *Pray,* then see if you can agree on setting three goals for the church:

one immediate: something to do this month;
one short-term: something to do this year;
one long-term: something to do in five years.

8
Make disciples

Too much evangelism stops at 'conversion'. Evangelistic rallies are arranged and the evangelist gives the appeal; twenty or thirty come forward, and this is repeated for several nights. But a year later only a handful of the hundred or more who 'came forward' can be found actually discipled into the church. Church Growth focuses attention on *Matthew 28:19 and the emphasis, not on producing converts, but on making disciples*.

Discipleship thinking is concerned to see people discipled into a local congregation. It is very difficult to produce any neat description of precisely what takes place in conversion, but it is quite clear that conversion involves both conversion *from* and conversion *to*. The Christians at Thessalonica turned *from* idols *to* God (1 Thessalonians 1:9).

Scripture also makes it clear that conversion is not merely a temporary phenomenon. Becoming a Christian is not something that one has a go at 'to see if it works'. It is not like an inoculation which might or might not 'take'. Conversion in biblical terms involves a complete change of mind (repentance, Greek *metanoia*, means just that, not merely being sorry). Conversion means leaving one way of life and setting out on a new way. It means being 'born again'.

It is this idea of being 'born again' that suggests most clearly that genuine conversion cannot be followed by a relapse into unbelief, a return to being *not* born again. Probably every Christian experiences times when he doubts almost everything. Temporary doubts and real ups and downs in Christian experience are to be expected, but not a deliberate abandoning of allegiance to Christ.

We are, however, often perplexed by numbers of 'converts' who do turn back or give up. Some simply fade away soon after the evangelistic rally at which they 'went forward'. A few drop out even after years of apparent walking with God. In such cases I should want to say that there never was a genuine new birth, a real *metanoia*, a new mind. New resolutions, perhaps, but all such resolutions necessarily prove inadequate in the long haul.

The crux experience

And it seems to me that there is often, usually, and perhaps always, a crux experience which marks the decisive break between the old and the new. It could be the act of going forward or signing some kind of card, or even confirmation or baptism. Unfortunately these are very often *not* crux experiences.

The crux experience is an experience which decisively cuts a person off from his old way of life and commits him to walking with Christ. To be a genuine crux experience it must obviously somehow involve whatever powers or situations or people that have dominated the person's life hitherto.

Someone who has always simply followed whatever his mates at work have done needs a crux experience which will show his mates that he is now abandoning their lead to follow someone else. When I was a young student at evening classes, two of us decided to pray definitely for the conversion of another student. One Sunday it happened. He became a Christian. The next day, when he came to lectures, he arrived with an outsize Bible which he ostentatiously set down on the desk in front of him. That was his crux experience, his way of telling the rest, 'I'm with the Jesus group now.'

Not too long ago a new house fellowship was started on an estate where there was no church. Janet (not her real name) turned up and eventually she bought herself a Bible. It was a Good News Bible, with its bright yellow jacket. It embarrassed her to be seen on that estate, carrying a Bible, so each Sunday she carefully wrapped it up and tucked it in her bag before setting off for church. One Sunday she walked in smiling. 'What have you been up to?' 'Well, I was just coming out of the house and I suddenly thought, Oh, blow 'em. What does it matter if they see I'm a Christian? So I took the Bible out of the bag and put it under me arm.' That was *her* crux decision.

We have several examples of crux decisions in the Bible. In the Old Testament Gideon was told to destroy the altar which his father had constructed for the worship of Baal. Beside it there was a tree, an *Asherah,* which represented the Canaanite goddess of fertility. Gideon had to cut it down (Judges 6:25–27). This was his crux experience. After doing that, there was really no possibility of Gideon going back to the worship of the Canaanite gods.

In the New Testament we have the example of the rich young man who wanted eternal life (Mark 10:17–22). Jesus told him to sell all that he had, to give the money to the poor and to follow him. That was his crux. He couldn't do it, couldn't face it. He went back into the old life.

Education for discipleship

Discipleship thinking expects a crux experience, but doesn't leave matters there. The new Christian has to be discipled; he has to learn what is involved in following Christ. He has to learn about prayer. Prayer doesn't just come naturally. Jesus' own followers had to ask him to teach them to pray. The new Christian has to learn how to read his Bible: when to read it, what to read, how to understand it, where to find books that will help him to understand it.

Again, we have already seen the need for a Christian Education programme in the church, and that programme ought to include a place for the new Christian. We have to learn that our task of being witnesses brings results, but that discipling is a continuing process, being changed, as the Bible puts it, from one degree of glory to another. Continuously. Right through life.

We have not finished with this question of discipleship, though. Church Growth thinking challenges the idea that we have about conversion as being a one-by-one matter. In the western world we tend to be individualists, where everyone does his own thing. And we expect people to be brought to Christ in the same way, one by one. But it does not always happen that way.

Right at the beginning of Donald McGavran's thinking about Church Growth he was concerned with the problem of new converts who became Christians one by one, and one by one were isolated from their community by being transferred into the community of the missionaries. He could see that the one-by-one expectations of the missionaries determined the results. But he also recognized that the Bible does not, in fact, prescribe any particular pattern of conversion.

Certainly there are plenty of examples of individual conversions: Candace's Treasurer (Acts 8:26–40), Paul. But there is also the mass movement on the day of Pentecost, when 3,000 were added to the church. As a consequence of Peter's preaching, the people who lived along the coastal plain of Sharon and the inhabitants of Lydda *all* turned to the Lord (Acts 9:35). In Acts 16 we find that the entire family of the Philippian jailer was converted.

Church Growth thinking emphasizes the significance of these varied patterns of conversion: *Christians come to Christ in many different ways, sometimes individually, sometimes in groups.*

Where a family becomes a Christian family the individuals are able to help each other. It does make good biblical sense to preach to families. This may be done through family services (and if the children are to be present, then a thirty-minute sermon is *not* called for). It could be through visiting (can we drop the word 'visitation', I wonder? The word is archaic, but still suggests to me some kind of plague!). Best of all, witness *to* a family is made most effectively *by* a family. Again, it is amazing to find whole families being prepared for just this step of faith.

An Evangelism Explosion team arranged to visit a home known to one of the team members. The mother had two children. Her husband had died. She had rather vague Roman Catholic connections. When the team arrived she was waiting for them, although there was no sign of the elder boy (let us call him David); he was upstairs. 'He's an atheist. He's not interested in religion.' They talked for about an hour and then called a halt for a cup of coffee. At which point David came downstairs, but not to mock at them. 'I knew what you would be talking about, and I've already got beyond that point,' he said. Entirely unknown to his mother, David had already been seeking God, talking with Christians. Today, both children and their mother are discipled into a fine Anglican church.

We may not be able to describe exactly what is happening when God calls groups into his family. Ultimately, of course, each individual has his own personal dealings with God. But there can be no doubt of the reality and of the biblical validity of groups who turn to God together.

THE CHRISTIAN EDUCATION PROGRAMME

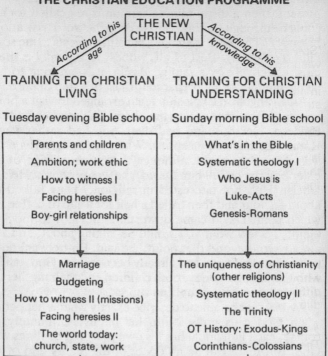

THE NEW CHRISTIAN

According to his age

According to his knowledge

TRAINING FOR CHRISTIAN LIVING	TRAINING FOR CHRISTIAN UNDERSTANDING
Tuesday evening Bible school	Sunday morning Bible school
Parents and children Ambition; work ethic How to witness I Facing heresies I Boy-girl relationships	What's in the Bible Systematic theology I Who Jesus is Luke-Acts Genesis-Romans
Marriage Budgeting How to witness II (missions) Facing heresies II The world today: church, state, work	The uniqueness of Christianity (other religions) Systematic theology II The Trinity OT History: Exodus-Kings Corinthians-Colossians
Divorce and counselling How to witness III (preaching) Church history: an overview Problems of ageing	The church and church government Systematic theology III The sacraments John's five books Isaiah

The programme allows for alternate weeks for games, including table games. Worship and refreshments are a regular feature.

The programme allows for the preparation of plays and other presentations by one group to the rest.

NOW WHAT DO WE DO?

Planning a Christian Education programme

Let us take Colossians 1:28–29 as our starting-point: 'So we preach Christ to everyone. With all possible wisdom we warn and teach them in order to bring each one into God's presence as a mature individual in union with Christ. To get this done I toil and struggle, using the mighty strength which Christ supplies and which is at work in me' (Good News Bible).

So the goal of the Christian Education programme is to bring all Christians to maturity. But it is evident that the goal is not easily reached. We need three things: people, courses and resources.

1. People

You cannot effectively *teach* people in the mass. They need to be divided into groups with common needs. Of course there are some needs that we *all* have, and those subjects can be dealt with when the whole church comes together. But teenagers do have different problems from the problems of the middlies, and so on.

2. Courses

The courses of study must be *relevant* to the people. Frankly, this is why most people do not come to Bible study meetings, because the studies are not relevant: they don't help you on Thursday morning.

The courses, however, must be *biblical,* though not necessarily studying, say, First Timothy. But what is taught should not just be picked off the radio or TV. All human knowledge is in the process of change, but the Bible is not like that. It is a sure guide, a straight line against which we can measure the crookedness of much that is taught by the media. So what is taught in the churches must be biblical, that is, in agreement with Scripture.

The courses must be *interesting.* They should naturally be interesting if they are relevant, but a dull teacher can make even the most relevant course as dull as an empty filing-cabinet. An interesting course will use visual aids and will involve the audience actively.

3. Resources

Most churches complain that they cannot run a full educational programme because they do not have the resources. Try this. Join the nine spots with four straight lines without taking your pen off the paper:

```
•  •  •
•  •  •
•  •  •
```

It *can* be done! But it cannot be done without extending the lines outside the limits of the square. Now I have not said that the problem must be solved by drawing lines which do not go beyond the square. Most people, when they try to solve the problem, simply *assume* that they cannot go outside the square.

It is the same way with the church. Most churches *do not have* sufficient resources within the church to mount a satisfactory Christian Education programme, so they assume that they cannot have one and that the problem cannot be solved. It can.

External resources are of two kinds: resources we can bring into the church and resources we can take the church to. So when we are *sure* that we have tapped all the resources *inside* the church, then we can look outside: to other churches in the area; to Christians who are prepared to come to the church in order to teach in their own specialties, such as lecturers in universities, Bible colleges, teachers of Religious Studies in schools; to organizations that are willing to run courses, such as the Bible Society, Maranatha Ministries, the Evangelical Alliance. And what about teaching cassettes? 'Highlights in church history' from the International Correspondence Institute is an excellent example of what is available. And surely *someone* is going to start producing Christian video cassettes soon…. And don't overlook the resources of the local library.

But do not forget the resources available outside your own church: courses being taught in evening institutes, for example on Islam or Buddhism or Marxism. And often there are useful Bible studies and lectures being held in other churches. The local Council will sometimes arrange a series of lectures on the social services. And both the old steam radio as well as TV continue from time to time to put out factual programmes (but beware of the twisted ones, the less-than-honest ones, the make-a-point-at-any-price programmes).

4. How to start

Start with the resources you have got. Have a small group produce a list of, say, *twenty* subjects which *they* think are relevant to the church, and then allow church members and others interested to select which ones they want. A check-list on paper is the best way; otherwise, if it is done by a show of hands, people will vote for what they *ought* to want instead of what they *do* want. (At one church they took two votes on the same list. The first vote was 'hands up' and the second was by written ballot. 'Prayer' came first in priority in the 'hands up' vote, but *last* on the written ballot!)

Choose, say, *three* of the top six subjects and offer them all on the same evening, and have people *sign up* for the course they want to attend.

Keep your small education study group going, planning to expand the programme as needs become more apparent.

5. Something to read

You might start with chapter 9 of Gavin Reid's *The gagging of God.*

Postscript:
This is where we're going

Church Growth: not a system, nor a method, but a movement of those who are concerned to see the church getting a clear idea of its principal task once again, concerned to see the gifts of the Spirit used by the Spirit, to see all God's people involved in God's work.

The church in the United Kingdom is waking up out of long years of slumber. The people outside of the churches are disillusioned: they know that life without God does not make sense, and the golden age has never happened. A new opportunity is here. I believe that Church Growth thinking, led by the Spirit through the Word, can help us all, in every kind of church, to meet the marvellous possibilities in front of us.

I have outlined in this book eight of the principles of the Church Growth movement. So far as I know there is nothing that requires us to stop there, but these eight do seem to encapsulate the thinking of the movement.

Maybe you are wondering what is so revolutionary about Church Growth. I would agree: it is simply sound biblical thinking, but expressed in a fresh way so that we can see once again what the church is all about. It is a call to the church to assess all that it is doing in the light of the priority that Christ himself gave to the church, to make disciples and to be his witnesses.

There is no accompanying guarantee that where the principles are followed hundreds will come to Christ. But there is the certainty that the way of the Lord will be cleared of a great deal of rubbish, leaving him, through his Spirit, to move when and where he wills.

Appendix:
But this I don't believe

Because I do believe in the authority of Scripture and in the sovereignty of the Holy Spirit, there are some things in Church Growth thinking *as some people present it* that I cannot accept. I do not think that these particular ideas are essential to the Church Growth movement, but I do think that a lot of people are unnecessarily put off thinking in Church Growth terms because of them. So here is an attempt to clear away some of the confusion produced by unbiblical thinking. And the first idea is that of the so-called homogeneous unit (or HU).

The homogeneous unit explained
We can study the homogeneous unit only if we understand exactly what it is, but those in Church Growth circles who use the term do not usually define it adequately. For example, the Pasadena Consultation of June 1977, which was supposed to explore the idea of the HU in detail, made use of Dr McGavran's definition: 'A section of society in which all members have some characteristic in common.' The common characteristic was then further described as geographical or ethnic, linguistic, social, educational, vocational or economic, or some combination of these or

other factors. But this simply is not a definition at all. The power of a definition lies in its ability to *exclude,* but this 'definition' cannot exclude. *Any* crowd has *something* in common. By such a definition any crowd watching a football match is an HU. The entire population of Britain is an HU. The world population of women is an HU.

Let us explain what an HU is by an example. Consider a tennis club. The reason for forming the tennis club is to enable the members to play tennis. But that is not all. After all, they can play tennis, like everyone else, on the tennis-courts of the local council. However, those courts are not particularly well maintained, and were not very well made in the first place, and they always seem to be fully booked up just when you want to play. What is more, you have to suffer the inconvenience of all kinds of people *trying* to play tennis, whose tennis-balls go flying everywhere pursued by their owners who obviously get in the way of the serious players. There is the annoyance of spectators gawking at you and, probably, making ribald comments just when you need to concentrate most. Then after the game there is nowhere to change, no place for a shower and no proper arrangements for refreshments.

The tennis club does not merely enable you to play tennis. It encourages *serious* tennis players.

It is important to keep the members of the tennis club happy. After all, they have had to pay a considerable sum to join the club. The annual membership fee is kept high to discourage the amateurs. Furthermore, to ensure peace and quiet, the club is out in the country. Land is a little bit less expensive and one can guarantee freedom from unwanted spectators, although, of course, it does mean that unless one owns a car one cannot really get there.

Mixed clubs bring problems: petty jealousies, disagreement over partners. Then the ladies get fed up with being flattened by the muscle-men. So let's make it a ladies' tennis club.

Now observe carefully the way in which the comfort of a certain group of tennis-playing ladies is being cared for: by a process of exclusion. No men. Car-owners only. With an adequate income. Tennis players only. Oh yes, and you can't just join: you must be recommended by a member and then be voted in by the rest of the club.

The result of all this exclusiveness is what tends to be a very stable group of people. They have common likes, a common way of life and come from a common social background. Increasing the *commonality,* the things shared by all members, tends to increase the stability of the group. A group with a high level of commonality, an atypically high level of commonality, might be termed a homogeneous unit.

Of course the group is *not* homogeneous. They will look different: blondes as well as brunettes, five-footers as well as a few six-footers, and all of different ages. But still the group does have an unusually high level of commonality, and this makes for a high level of group stability.

Now applying this observation to the church, the argument runs as follows: Stable groups are contented groups. Any local church is a group. It is desirable that the local congregation should be a contented group. If it is not a contented group then it will not grow. And so the local church should be a homogeneous unit, a group of Christians with an unusually high level of commonality.

The homogeneous unit under examination

I cannot quarrel with the sociological observations. The stability of a group which has a high level of commonality must be accepted. 'A cross-cultural community will not, usually, have a high level of commonality and it *will* have all kinds of tensions within it. But *why* does the HU have this stability? And why is the cross-cultural group unstable?

The instability, the arguments, the fighting, the competition – these are all to be explained by the Christian doctrine of the Fall. This is no mere myth, but a painful reality. We cannot live at peace with other people because of our fallen natures. We cannot think beyond *me* and *my*. 'What about *me*?' To go back to the tennis club: the tennis players who happily go down to the Council courts on a Saturday morning are not particularly interested in the obvious pleasure *other* people get out of playing. What about *me*? *I* want to play. And those who start their own tennis clubs do so out of primarily selfish motives.

Notice in particular the special characteristic of the HU: its ability to *exclude*. It allows the elect in, but deliberately keeps others out. The exclusion has in mind the selfish preferences of those who are in.

In the context of the non-Christian society such exclusiveness is entirely understandable. What I simply cannot understand is the attempt to import the behaviour of fallen society into the church. The reason is that this particular idea emerges from sociology, not from Scripture. True enough, the textbooks which promote the HU are sprinkled with supposed proof-texts in an attempt to legitimize the idea. But this aspect of Church Growth emerges from sociology and it is unbiblical.

The legitimate use of the idea of the HU

The HU, or more accurately the group with a high level of commonality, is a reality. It is necessarily found in unredeemed society, and since evangelism must take place in unredeemed society it is apparent that *evangelism* ought to take note of the role of the HU. Evangelism always involves reaching across cultural barriers and, as we have seen, people ought not to be asked to cross unnecessary cultural barriers in coming to Christ. Evangelism from within an HU could very well make sense.

We owe the very convenient terminology of cross-cultural evangelism to Ralph Winter. He points out that cross-cultural evangelism becomes more and more difficult as the separation between the cultures increases. His system has become more and more cumbersome as new sub-divisions have been added, but let us take here the simplest outline, with E1, E2 and E3 types.

E1 evanglism is the English John Churchman witnessing to English people who are not Christians. E2 evangelism is

John witnessing to French people who are not Christians. E3 evangelism is John going to Pakistan to witness to non-Christians.

It is not difficult to see that we might add all kinds of sub-divisions: if John lives in London but goes off to Newcastle to be a witness, he will find the fisher-folks of Cullercoats very different from his London neighbours. Or he might try witnessing to Pakistanis living in Birmingham. But we can see the general outline of Ralph Winter's scheme.

In evangelism it is 'easiest' to witness at the E1 level. Because of the problems of language in particular and culture in general John finds E3 evangelism difficult. He has no trouble with English, a little more with his French, but his Urdu is poor. Of course even in England he might find his *dialect* something of a problem in communicating the Good News. And that is why a vicar who has done well in his native Birmingham comes a cropper when he is promoted to Chelsea.

What we are suggesting here is that in *evangelism* the idea of the HU is useful, precisely because we are dealing with people who share in the general fallen condition of all men. They would have no motivation that might make them give up *their* way of doing things just to make other people comfortable: 'If you don't like it you can lump it.' They respond best to witnesses who come from their own background. They would be likely to 'turn off' other witnesses.

But when people become Christians, when they *join* a local congregation, they have to learn a new way of life. They must learn biblical ideas which are *not* exclusive. In the church *all* are welcome.

The New Testament church
So we must look at the New Testament picture of the church. In fact, we shall do this in two ways: by looking at the New Testament description of groups of Christians, and then we shall look at the theology of the New Testament *about* these groups.

The church at Antioch makes a good starting-point. When the church in Jerusalem was persecuted the Christians were scattered and some of them reached Antioch. A church was started. In Acts 13 we are given a list of the prophets and teachers of the church. Five are named and a more obviously non-homogeneous lot it would be difficult to find. There was Barnabas, a Jewish Levite from Cyprus. There was Saul, a Jew, but from the tribe of Benjamin and from Tarsus. Simeon is nicknamed Niger, 'black', and was probably, like Lucius of Cyrene, from North Africa. Finally there was Manaen, probably an Idumaean, like Herod Antipas to whom he was in some way related. But what a mixture!

A very striking example of the church as a non-HU is the church at Corinth. This church had many problems. Some of its problems arose from the very fact that it was *not* a homogeneous unit. From 1 Corinthians 11 we find that real difficulty was being caused by the existence within the one church of wealthy Christians and poor Christians. There were some who 'had nothing' and there were others who had quite enough to eat and more than enough to drink. The result was painful. Apparently the church had adopted the local custom of a kind of pot-luck supper. Everyone brought his evening meal and they pooled what was brought. But there was not always enough of the meat and wine brought by the wealthy to go round. Sometimes they were reduced to eating the bread brought by the poor members. And so the church split, with everyone eating his own meal.

But what is so important for us is the fact that, although the problem so obviously arose at Corinth because the church was a mixture of rich and poor, Paul did *not* give the church the advice that would square with the HU principle. He might have said: 'Your problem is apparent, the cause is obvious. What you need is two churches, not one.' But he did not say that. He did not suggest that two churches would solve the problem, and they could get over the danger of an openly divided church by coming together for a good sing once a month. Instead he pointed to the obvious fact of God's displeasure: some were ill, some had even died. Paul insisted that the believers *must* recognize the *whole* body of Christ, *all* its members. He expected the Christians to have the resources to break down the social barriers. 'But I just can't do it! I can't get on with that lot!' The New Testament would say that you must. For if the church cannot break down the barriers between rich and poor, black and white, old and young, then who can?

And now let us look at the theology of the thing. The classical passage in the New Testament on the subject of Christian unity must be Ephesians 2:11–22. Paul is writing to a church which included within itself both Jews and non-Jews. He reminds the Gentiles, the non-Jews, of what they had been: without God and without hope, natural enemies of the Jews. But now, says Paul,

> '... he is our peace, who has made us both one, and has broken down the dividing wall of hostility, by abolishing in his flesh the law of commandments and ordinances, that he might create in himself one new man in place of the two, so making peace, and might reconcile us both to God in one body through the cross, thereby bringing the hostility to an end' (verses 14–16).

Paul insists that the most pernicious of sociological divisions, the division between Jew and Gentile, that division which has given rise to centuries of anti-Semitism and to the horrors of the holocaust, that division has, for the Christian, been abolished.

In Galatians 3 Pauls shows that in Christ a new family is created to which the categories of unredeemed society simply do not apply:

> '... in Christ Jesus you are all sons of God, through faith. For as many of you as were baptized into Christ have put on Christ. There is neither Jew nor Greek [ethnic differences gone], there is neither slave nor free

117

[social differences gone], there is neither male nor female *[sex discrimination gone]; for you are all one in Christ Jesus'* (verses 26–28).

And Paul has the same message for the Christians at Colossae (3:11).

We might want to reply pragmatically: 'Let's be practical. These barriers are real. We can't deny the problems that emerge when you have people from all kinds of cultural backgrounds mixed together. They just don't get on. It's asking for trouble.' The New Testament would respond: 'I'm sorry. It is the genius of the Good News that it nullifies those barriers of which you speak. Your failure to break down the barriers raises a question-mark over the reality of the Good News. If you can't demonstrate the power of the gospel by crossing those barriers which so obviously owe their existence to mistrust, suspicion and human pride, then how do you propose to demonstrate it?'

The tyranny of the seven vital signs

I cannot accept the concept of the homogeneous unit as providing the pattern for the local church. And yet this has been stated to be one of the vital signs of a growing church: that it *is* a homogeneous unit, that the members come almost exclusively from a single social class.

I was asked to talk about Church Growth to a group of young Christians. In the course of my talk I was describing a certain church which I had recently visited. In fact I had not only visited the church, but had spent a weekend with them at an away-day. I had been very impressed by the mixed congregation that they had: it appeared to be almost equally divided between immigrants, most of them from the West Indies, and umpteenth-generation Londoners. They seemed to have crossed the class barrier, too. True enough, there were no upper-crust nobility to be seen, but then *they* do not live in East London. Investigation showed that this was a *growing* church. But the young people to whom I was talking had read their Church-Growth books:

118

'But that church *can't* be growing. It's not a homogeneous unit. Being an HU is one of the seven vital signs of a growing church.'

Some writers on Church Growth refer to a number of vital signs, signs which indicate a growing church. Some few even go so far as to suggest that unless these signs are present a church *cannot* grow. But this I cannot accept, because of my two basic presuppositions: the authority of Scripture and the sovereignty of the Spirit. If I understand God's omnipotence correctly, *anything* can happen.

The nature of the 'vital signs' and even their number vary, but here is probably the most authoritative set, from Dr Peter Wagner of Fuller Theological Seminary's Institute of Church Growth:

1. The church must have a dynamic pastor who expects growth and plans for it, and is able to enthuse his congregation for it.
2. The church must have its members actively engaged in the work of the church, with the spiritual gifts actively employed.
3. The church must be a large one, able to provide for all the varied needs of its members.
4. The church will be using G2, G3 and G4 meetings (although Wagner does not use this terminology, nor describe his groups quite as I have done).
5. The membership of the congregation must be drawn primarily from a single homogeneous unit.
6. The church must make use of methods of evangelism which have already been shown in a similar context to be effective, fully deploying the 10% of the church who have the gift of evangelism.
7. The church must observe a biblical priority for its activities, specifically putting evangelism before social action.

These seven vital signs are a very mixed lot, of very differing significance, and no one of them would seem to me to be a *necessary* indicator of a growing church. In fact, a 1979 survey of Baptist churches in Britain reported negatively on the seven signs.

But we should not dismiss the seven signs altogether. It is true that, for better or for worse, the minister of a church plays a major role in any programme of outreach. It is hard to get things going if he will not budge. And similarly it *is* important, as we have seen, to get the church members involved in the work of the church, so that all of the gifts of the Spirit can be put to use by the Spirit.

Rather than the three group sizes indicated by Dr Wagner, I would want to think of the four sizes I have described, with particular attention paid to the two groups at the ends of the series: G1 and G4. Much more attention needs to be given to the need of older people and the young people for a Christian *family* experience. And much more needs to be done to provide for what Dr Wagner calls *Celebration,* the joyous coming together of a large number of Christians to *worship*.

In fact we seem, in Britain, to have lost the experience of *worship* altogether. In most non-conformist churches people no longer turn up to the traditional mid-week meeting for Bible study, so if the minister is going to do any serious Bible teaching it has to be done on Sunday. The result is that everything but the sermon is lumped together and labelled *the preliminaries,* while the thirty-minute sermon becomes the focus of the gathering. Few Christians go to church because it is enjoyable and stimulating. Too often the service is a chore to get through.

But many churches are moving to a new concept. The *sermon* is removed from the worship service altogether. The whole church comes together at 10.30, say, for its Christian Education programme, in groups, with classes and real teaching for all. Then at 11.15, say, everyone moves into the main church for worship. There is no sermon, no collection and no notices, for these have all been disposed of earlier. Parents do not have to cope with fidgety children, because the children can singalong with the rest. And attention really can be focused on the hymns and prayers so as to usher in a spirit of real worship: the proper response to the realization of God's presence.

The Engel Scale

I do not believe in the homogeneous unit church and I do not believe in seven vital signs without which a church *cannot* be growing, and I do not believe in this Engel Scale, which attempts to indicate just how far from conversion a person is by reference to his present beliefs about God:

−10	He has only an awareness of the existence of a Supreme Being.
−9	He believes in the existence of a Personal God.
−8	He has some awareness of the Christian gospel.
−7	He is ready to accept the channel being used to show him the nature of the Good News.
−6	He is aware of a personal need, though this may be ill-defined.
−5	He has grasped the implications of the Good News.
−4	He is thinking positively about the Good News, not actively rejecting it, but seriously considering it.
−3	He recognizes that he has a *personal* problem, and that he cannot deal with the problem by himself.
−2	He decides to act on what he knows about the gospel.
−1	He repents and puts his trust in Christ.
0	He becomes a new creation.

Whatever the intentions of Engel when he formulated the scale, it is inevitable that the scale will suggest something that is quite unbiblical, that the man who scores minus ten is further from God than the man who scores minus three. But that is not so. Both are equally dead, both are equally unsaved. There is no certainty that either will, in fact, come to Christ, nor any likelihood at all that the minus three man will come to faith in Christ before the minus ten man. Nor does one have to slide down the scale from minus ten to minus nine and so on, gradually passing through each supposed stage until at last the moment of conversion is reached. Even a decision to act, at minus two, is not the same as action, and all of us know of people who are quite decided to act... but never get any further.

The only use of the Engel scale might be as an indicator of how I might speak to a particular person to whom I was trying to be Christ's witness. But even here there is real danger of the introduction of a mechanical approach, passing through the ten or so stages in the expectation that when at last the end is reached the person *must* be saved. The Holy Spirit of God, not a mechanical system, must lead us in our privilege of witnessing for Christ.

Reading and resources

Eddie Gibbs' *I believe in Church Growth* (Hodder and Stoughton 1981) provides a more detailed discussion of many of the points raised in this book and is strongly recommended.

Church growth

Gibbs, Eddie, *Body-building exercises for the local church* (Falcon, 1979).

Gibbs, Eddie, *Urban church growth* (Grove Booklet No. 55) (Grove Books, 1977).

Goldsmith, Martin, *Can my church grow?* (Hodder, 1980).

Harper, Michael, *Let my people grow* (Hodder, 1977).

McGavran, Donald and Winfield Arn, *Ten steps for church growth* (Harper & Row, 1977, available from Evangelical Alliance, Whitefield House, 186 Kennington Park Road, London SE11 4BT).

Nationwide Initiative in Evangelism, *Prospects for the Eighties* (Bible Society, 1980).

Thomson, Robin, *Can British churches grow?* (Bible and Medical Missionary Fellowship, n.d.).

The Bible Society (146 Queen Victoria Street, London EC4V 4BX) runs day and weekend courses on church growth, congregation profiles, *etc.*

The Evangelical Alliance (Whitefield House, 186 Kennington Park Road, London SE11 4BT) has its own Church Growth Unit, which published the *Church Growth Digest*.

Maranatha Ministries (32 Smithy Lane, Tadworth, Surrey KT20 6TX) operate Church Growth seminars, especially in the South of England.

Groups, communication, management
Bion, W. R., *Experiences in groups* (Tavistock Publications, 1968).

Copley, Derek, *Home Bible studies and how to run them* (Paternoster, 1972).

Copley, Derek and Nancy, *Building with bananas* (Paternoster, 1978).

Drucker, Peter F., *The practice of management* (Pan, 1968).

Gibbs, Eddie, *Grow through groups* (Grove Booklet No. 64) (Grove Books, 1979).

Osmaston, Amiel, *Sharing the life: using small groups in the church* (Grove Booklet No. 63) (Grove Books, 1979).

Sprott, W. J. H., *Human groups* (1958; reissued Penguin, 1970).

Word alive! (a booklet on leading group Bible studies, available from UCCF).

Evangelism
Green, Michael, *Evangelism – now and then* (IVP, 1979).

Little, Paul, *How to give away your faith* (IVP, 1971).

Pippert, Rebecca Manley, *Out of the saltshaker* (IVP, 1980).

Reid, Gavin, *The gagging of God* (Hodder, 1969).

Reid, Gavin, *Good news to share* (Falcon, 1979).

Sheppard, David, *Built as a city* (Hodder, 1974).

Stott, John, *Our guilty silence* (Hodder, 1967).

Walker, Tom, *Open to God: a parish in renewal* (Grove Booklet No. 38) (Grove Books, 1975).

Christian life and discipleship
Griffiths, Michael, *Take my life* (IVP, 1967).

Milne, Bruce, *We belong together* (IVP, 1978).

White, John, *The cost of commitment* (IVP, 1976).

White, John, *The fight* (IVP, 1977).

Spiritual gifts
Bridge, Donald and David Phypers, *Spiritual gifts and the church* (IVP, 1973).
Griffiths, Michael, *Cinderella with amnesia* (IVP, 1975).
Griffiths, Michael, *Cinderella's betrothal gifts* (OMF, 1978).

Worship and prayer
Anderson, Jock, *Worship the Lord* (IVP, 1980).
Long, Anne, *Praise him in the dance* (Hodder, 1976).
White, John, *People in prayer* (IVP, 1978).
Several publishers have produced books of prayers for use both in private and publicly.

Music
Psalm praise (CPAS, 1973).
Pulkingham, Betty and Jeanne Harper, *Sound of living waters* (Hodder, 1975).
Pulkingham, Betty and Jeanne Harper, *Fresh sounds* (Hodder, 1976).
Sing Good News (Bible Society, 1980).
Songs of worship (Scripture Union, 1980).
With thanksgiving (Mustard Seed Recordings, 36 Mill Lane, Heworth, York YO3 7TE. 4th ed., 1979).

Teaching programme
Daily Bible Commentary and *Daily Bible Study Books* (Scripture Union) are two series which help to explain and apply the Bible in a down-to-earth way.
I want to know what the Bible says... (Kingsway) is a series covering the understanding and applying of basic Christian teaching.
Key Books (Scripture Union) include such titles as Paul Little's *Know what you believe* and John Stott's *Understanding the Bible.*
Understanding Bible teaching (Scripture Union) is a series of paperbacks directing Christians to the Bible's teaching on fundamental Christian truths.

Study and resource material

Burbridge, Paul and Murray Watts, *Time to act* (Hodder, 1979).

Cotterell, Peter, *What next?* (Lakeland, 1979) is a study/ideas book for new Christians.

Davies, Chris, Brede Kristensen and Ada Lum, *Jesus – one of us* (IVP, 1981) is a book of evangelistic Bible studies on the person of Christ; also useful for young Christians.

Fisherfolk Kits. Various drama kits are available from Celebration Services (Post Green) Ltd, 57 Dorchester Road, Lytchett Minster, Poole, Dorset BH16 6JE.

Grow together. Adult group study material edited by Margaret Old (published quarterly by Scripture Union).

New beginnings. A Bible study booklet for new Christians to use in groups (available from UCCF).

Ready, steady... Group Bible studies in preparation for evangelism (available from UCCF).

The Bible Society produces a range of group study material at different levels and for different groups (available from 146 Queen Victoria Street, London EC4V 4BX), especially *Prospects for the Eighties,* an invaluable collection of church statistics, published in 1980.

Celebration Services produce study courses for church groups (57 Dorchester Road, Lytchett Minster, Poole, Dorset BH16 6JE).

Falcon produces a variety of audio-visual aids for use with groups (obtainable from Falcon Court, 32 Fleet Street, London EC4Y 1DB). Note in particular the workbooks for evangelism and a series of teaching cassettes by David Watson.

Scripture Union's audio-visual department also has a useful list of material for groups (130 City road, London EC1V 2NJ).

UCCF produces a whole series of notes and outlines for group Bible studies on books of the Bible and on topics (38 De Montfort Street, Leicester LE1 7GP).

Urban Church Project has a series of articles on church groups, especially relevant to the Church of England (available from David Wasdell, St Matthias Vicarage, Poplar High Street, London E1 0AE).

Practical matters
Managing a church bookstall (Hodder, 1980).
Publicity material is available from CPO, Ivy Arch Road, Worthing, E. Sussex BN14 8BU.
Overhead projector materials are available from commercial stationers or educational suppliers.